D0008276

LEAVING HOME

LEAVING HOME

EVELYN BENCE

TYNDALE HOUSE
Publishers, Inc.
Wheaton, Illinois

First printing, January 1986
Library of Congress Catalog Card Number 85-51595
ISBN 0-8423-2129-2
Copyright © 1986 by Evelyn Bence
All rights reserved
Printed in the United States of America

155.6423

B457l

c.1

TO ALL WHO HAVE GONE BEFORE

CONTENTS

ACKNOWLEDGMENTS

"Deliverance" is reprinted by permission of *Today's Christian Woman* magazine, copyright © 1982, Fleming H. Revell.

"Business Trip to Cape Cod," "While gurgling a jar of applesauce," and "Home Sweet Nothing" first appeared in *The Poet.*

"The Day the Hope Died" first appeared in *Christianity and Literature* under the title "The Evolution of a Dream."

"On Wednesday's Faith on Tuesday" and "Engagement Announcements from College Friends" were previously published in *Solo*, The Christian Magazine for Single Adults.

The vignette in Chapter 9 first appeared in *Christian Herald* under the title "The Call."

The quotations from Chaplain Henry T. Close are reprinted with permission from Vicki Lansky's *Practical Parenting* newsletter, copyright © 1981 by Vicki Lansky.

Selections from *Once My Child . . . Now My Friend* are reprinted by permission of Warner Books/New York from *Once My Child . . . Now My Friend*, copyright © 1981 by Elinor Lenz.

Diligent effort has been made to locate and secure permission for the inclusion of all copyrighted material in this book. If any such acknowledgments have been inadvertently omitted, or if such were not received by the time of publication, the editor and publisher would appreciate receiving full information so that proper credit may be given in future editions.

FOREWORD

Parents and siblings. We love them and hate them. When with them, we feel confined; when away from them, we don't know exactly who we are. We want their eternal support but without any accompanying bondage. Although we want to be a part of them we leave them in search of what is ours and not theirs.

The journey away from them begins within seconds of our birth when life forces us to inhale. We take possession of the oxygen in our lungs or we die. From that moment we walk toward responsibility for our own lives. In childhood and adolescence we take baby steps toward independence. Without much trauma we learn to feed ourselves, walk, speak our minds, read, balance a bicycle, maneuver a car. Our parents or teachers show us what to do and we follow their example; we take the next difficult step toward self-sufficiency. Each new achievement—which they teach but which we must learn for ourselves—broadens our world and allows us to survive longer periods of time and lengthier distances away from them.

But then a day comes when the accumulation of years and lessons indicates that it is again time for a major departure, a birth into the world of adulthood.

Many women who come unmarried into this grown-up world know naturally how to breathe its air (physical survival depends on it), but they panic at learning the subsequent lessons that make for a satisfying or even tolerable independent life. The most difficult skills in this new life have little to do with adjusting physically to an alien world; this birth and growth are emotional—the womb of childhood is not erased from our consciousness. We remember the embracing security of the world we left behind and yearn to return to it for safety.

Yes, it is our memories that make this new world so difficult to face. We want to become like our mothers, yet we don't; we want to become like our fathers, but not really. We remember our parents' conflicting signals—their desire for us to grow up and fly from their nest, but their fear of that day ever dawning. Their desire for us to succeed, but their fear of our taking risks. Their desire for us to find a man and the security of his promises, but their fear of our being too aggressive in our search. Their desire for us to serve others, but their fear that we will be taken advantage of.

Our flight from home can be terrifying. Colette Dowling has commented: "Women are beginning to discover that nothing is more frightening than the escape into freedom" *(The Cinderella Complex)*. In leaving home we are forced to unlearn what our mothers have taught us about dependence and the importance of not making waves. And all for what? For a journey we still secretly hope will end where our mothers' journey started—as wives and then maybe as mothers.

We feel we must break away from the home of our childhood—for one reason or another it is no longer where we belong. But how much of that childhood should we take with us? Which parts of it must be discarded? Which parts of it must be slightly remolded and fitted into the home we make for ourselves? Which parts of it should stay completely intact and become integral parts of ourselves?

This book gives no *easy* answers to women, young or relatively young, who are walking away from the security of the home they have always known—the home of their parents— and toward a home they eventually will call their own. Finding out who we are and knowing what kind of home will provide us with the comfort we need to thrive can come only with the passing of time. Time that cannot be hurried, and time that must not be slept through.

Eventually we are able to define who we are, what our purpose is, what our contribution to humanity is. Our definitions become part of our new identity and home, but they must be broader-based than that: we must build bridges to the past, to the future, and to the people who surround us in the present.

In the pages of this book I attempt to peel apart, layer by layer, the years of transition between being a daughter and being one's own self, as one might peel apart an onion. I tell more than the story of my journey from the home of my parents to my own home, more than my birth into adulthood which took place the day I left for college (or was it the day I graduated, or the day my parents moved away from my "hometown"?). It is the stories of many independent women who have stepped away from the security of their families to establish a "family of one," and the stories of their building up the pilings that support the bridges that time, wind, or weather can never destroy.

The transition from dependence to independence can be made—successfully—and here is how.

I still cry every time I leave my parents' home.
A forty-year-old
career woman

PART
ONE

FAR FROM THE HOME I KNOW

ONE

🧳

LEAVE-TAKING

DELIVERANCE

It is time.
My body's clock gongs
your salvation's hour.
The water left the pasture and
has flowed toward the river's mouth.
Follow or you will wither
in the desert that remains.
I will bleed for you
on this, your first dark journey
but, in time, when life pushes you
headlong through black canyons
the wounds will become your own.
May you learn early
that at the end
there always shines light.
Breathe,
for therein lies your only hope.
It is here, child;
the time is come.

PARTIR C'EST MOURIR UN PEU. (To part is to die a little.)

French proverb

The ferry docked alongside its half-sunk ancestor, which had, in its day, carried millions of immigrants from Ellis Island to Manhattan. I looked up and thought I saw shadows of crying faces in the windows of the dilapidated buildings. Some eyes were shedding tears of joy or relief; those people were free and standing on the land of opportunity. Some eyes seemed desperate in their anguish.

The images faded as I walked off the boat and closer to the door of the main building. The voice of the crisply suited

U.S. Park Service guide welcomed me to the island once known for its harvest of oysters, now remembered for being a stop on people's way to somewhere else.

My thirteen-year-old niece accompanied me on my tour of Ellis Island. We both listened intently to stories of men and women losing their names and identities because of the language barrier and families losing their members because of improper papers or sickness.

"Anyone over twelve," the guide said, "who did not pass the physical was sent back to the old country—alone. Younger children were accompanied by one parent." The separations of families were what had caused this place to be called "the island of tears."

My niece was unusually quiet for the rest of the hour. On the return ferry ride she started to cry. "What's wrong?" I inquired.

"I would have been sent back to Europe, you know. Alone. And my family would have stayed in America."

"Yes," I responded. "Leaving is hard, even when you're older. But you're here and now and not there and then, so it's not something that you should worry about today. Why don't you just remember the story in a way that makes you more thankful for your family?"

And so the subject was dropped in conversation, but not in my thoughts. In five years, my niece no doubt would leave home to go to college, to get her own apartment, or to marry. By then she might be eager physically to move out, but where would her emotional home be? Would an ocean still seem like an infinite, impossible barrier? She might leave, a few miles or a few hundred miles at a time, and in so doing gradually lose hold of her family and/or her childhood identity. What kind of tears would she shed then? Joy at the prospect of freedom and adventure or sorrow at the loss of things past?

The morning I left for college the sun rose late, or so it seemed. I lay awake waiting for light to shine in around the pulled shade. I was excited about leaving. College was going to be fun, like one four-year-long summer camp. I would eat, clown, study, room with friends—never lack for someone to talk with. I would date, fall in love, fall out of love, until I found the man who would suit me, and I him. Then summer camp would be over and I would go home to a new house of my very own.

College was what I would have to walk through before stepping into life—the universe that revolved around me instead of around my parents. And at the time I was very willing to do what had to be done to get myself from one world to the next.

I had spent a week sorting and packing, and that morning I loaded the family Impala full of clothes, most of which I would never wear. On top of the skirts, dresses, and slacks that were stacked across the length of the backseat I threw the teddy bear that had sat for years in a chair in the corner of my bedroom, neglected. The more I emptied from my room, the less I wanted to leave behind.

The trip took two hours and during the second hour I grew more ambivalent, as did my parents. This sort of trip was nothing new for Father and Mother. I was the sixth child (the fifth daughter) they had transported to the transitory home of a college freshman dorm. But I remembered now, and only now, just one of those trips.

Thirteen years earlier, when my oldest sister had been driven to college, I had cried into my mother's lap the entire trip home. Even then I knew that things would never be the same. She was, in a sense, leaving home. As the youngest sister, I was moving from a cot in the boys' room into her half of one of the double beds in the girls' room. My clothes were replacing hers in the closet. She would be entering a life that we would know nothing about, unless she chose to tell us on weekend visits or in letters. Although I would think of her often and she would think of me, her physical presence and her voice would not be constant reminders of her being; I would know her only by memories, letters, and infrequent visits. Yet life went on without her.

And so it would go on for me, my parents, and my little brother, whom we had left at home. Their parsonage life together was going to function perfectly well without me, maybe even better than before. But I would miss not being in the midst of it.

My mother started saying that she would miss me and things like, "My little girl is going off to college." And for the last half hour of the trip I held her hand tightly.

We found my dorm room and, as quickly as possible, unpacked the car. Suitcases and boxes covered the gray tile floor. Suzanne, my roommate, welcomed me. My suite mates took a break from filling dresser drawers and warmly introduced themselves. By tomorrow, I assured myself, I would be a part of this new "family" of four who shared a common washroom.

But the time for saying good-bye to my parents came, and, as always at such moments, Father suggested that we pray before parting company. We huddled close to each other on the sidewalk next to the hood of the car. Again I held my mother's hand. Father prayed that I would remember all that they had taught me, that I would stay close to God. As he came to the part about God giving me the strength equal to my task, his voice broke. We were all crying at this my first major adult beginning and ending.

Why didn't I stop right then and there and say: "No, I'm not staying here. I'm too afraid of getting to know all these strangers. I'm afraid that it might all be too hard for me. I'm afraid that these people might not turn out to be the friends I was anticipating, but that I might find them annoying and irksome"?

As hard as it was for me to leave home, both my parents and I knew there was no going back; I simply had to trust my future to the knowledge and common sense gained in the past and to the God of my father's prayers. As fearful as that next step was, I knew I wanted to take it. I did want to begin a life of my own. A year earlier, when sickness in the family and the subsequent financial crisis had threatened my prospects for rooming and boarding at an out-of-town college, I had been horrified at the thought of missing out on dorm life. What was college, if not a social venture?

If I had demanded to return home I think my parents would not have let me come—just as they hadn't let me stay home from school on that first morning of kindergarten when I clutched my mother's knees and refused to walk up

the bus steps. There are times when one has no choice but to
move.

And so they left me, or I left them—physically, and more
permanently than any of us could know, for the only college
summer job I ever found was near the home of my brother,
one hundred miles away. I never again spent more than two
weeks at a time in their presence.

*All beginnings are hard. . . . Especially a beginning
that you make by yourself.*

Chaim Potok
IN THE BEGINNING

I hear other stories of women leaving home. Some left easily,
never looking back, relieved to be escaping some earthly
hell. Some called back home two weeks later saying, "Come
and get me." One cried for weeks during her second semes-
ter, although at the time she didn't know why. Some delayed
their grief of separation even further and did not feel the
break until their sophomore year. Some always kept the
thought forefront in their minds that this state of being
away was temporary, and so it proved to be. They went home
every weekend or phoned frequently to check in, and later
dropped out or transferred nearer home.

*I was happy as a lark at leaving home. I was sixteen
and filled with a sense of great independence. I was on
my own and no longer to be cared for by the family. . . .
It was not until a few months later, when the novelty
of my surroundings wore off, that I suffered from a
terrible homesickness which made me go to bed
weeping, wake up weeping, and which filled me with a
sense of desolation and loneliness. . . . I had a terrible
sense of loss and yet with it a sense of the inevitability
of such losses in our lives. It never occurred to me to
turn back. . . . It was a desolation to be worked
through, lived through, and even while I suffered I
knew that it would pass.*

Dorothy Day
THE LONG LONELINESS

Moving out does not mean that one has left home. I can't remember anyone referring to the dormitory or to a student residence as "home." It was "I'm going to the dorm," or "I'm going to the house." "I'm going home" was reserved for the place where family lived—just as if they were still at summer camp.

Dietrich Bonhoeffer describes homes as being "not, like the shelters of animals, merely the means of protection against bad weather . . . ; they are places in which a man may relish the joys of his personal life in the intimacy and security of his family and of his property" *(Ethics).*

The *Thorndike Barnhart Dictionary* defines "home" as a "place where a person can rest and be safe." My bedroom in my parents' house was still far more safe than my college room. The immediate, visible rooming houses sufficed as long as the knowledge of a home remained constant. Responsibility for keeping up my grades was not much different from high school. What I did with my time and whether or not I ate my meals were minor daily decisions that soon became old hat. I was my father's dependent. My bills would be paid, food would be available. Home, parents, and their responsibility for my livelihood were a phone call away.

The beginning of college years quickly turned into the middle years, and middles (never as hard as beginnings or endings) passed by smoothly. The pain and fear of separation were lessened by time and distraction. The books, the exams, the social life consumed the hours and the energy, with the goal of graduation seeming to be the end of all time.

I vividly remember leaning against the back end of a car parked in the lot outside my college dorm. I was in my junior year and going home for Christmas break. Suzanne, my best friend, stood with me. We were waiting for my parents. I don't remember which of us spoke but that doesn't seem important, because we both felt suddenly overwhelmed with the same sentiment: Something was changing. When we would come back, things wouldn't be the same. They would never be the same again. "I'm losing something," one of us said. We tried to analyze. What was leaving us? Why was its loss making us so depressed?

My parents arrived, and I went home with them for vacation. After New Year's I came back to campus, and although I didn't then try to figure out exactly what it was that had happened, I knew that our parking lot discussion had foretold what was indeed coming to pass. The security of childhood was falling out of the range of our reach. I started to glimpse proof that after college graduation one stepped into a shaky world made of gelatin. The more I saw the more I envisioned myself sinking waist-deep into a green gel—being able to breathe but not walk without help from some outside source.

So far the love of my life had not fallen in my lap, nor within sight or even shooting range, as I had most assuredly thought he would. The life schedule had called for the planning of a wedding by the end of my junior year.

Only God knows why, but I had chosen business administration as my major field. I certainly had no intention of having to prepare financial statements for the rest of my life. I intended to spend it making a home for myself and someone else. Isn't that what my mother had done? What most of my older sisters had done?

My senior year dawned. The religious college I attended prided itself in being a shoe factory—mending souls and sending them out in pairs. A student's senior year was one intense game called "search for your soul mate." The rules were flexible and the playing field was anywhere in the whole town—and beyond.

By October I knew for sure that I was losing at this game. Neither beauty nor a sweet disposition was on my side. Truth and sincerity, I knew, were. But such virtues never seemed to catch the eye of the beholder.

On one trip home that year Father asked me what I intended to do with my life. Not having any idea, really, yet having sat through untold hours of management courses, I told him I would rise to the top of some organization. I figured if I wasn't going to be successful at Mother's role, I would follow Father's steps; he had climbed up the church's administration ladder.

He looked at me grievedly. "A woman will never be given that kind of position."

He was speaking words of some foreign language. Women hadn't because they hadn't tried. I had never even contemplated the thought that the work world would differ one iota from the undergraduate world, at least as I had experienced it: if you are smart and if you work you are at the top of the class. And there is never any question but that someone at the top of the class is promoted. The thought that one's sex rather than one's ability or fortitude might have something to do with it made me ill.

"A woman's place," he said, "is in the home."

Oh, why did it have to come to this? I thought, but actually said something like, "But it doesn't seem to be working out that way. I have no husband; who will pay the rent?"

His last retort was killing. "It doesn't seem to me that you've been trying very hard."

He had no idea how hard I had been trying. If *he* thought I had devoted four years to successful studies, I thought I had devoted four years to failing at a woman's primary purpose. Although I had been desperate in my attention-getting antics, it never failed that, in the end, men shook my hand at the door and told me how great it was that I could be one of the gang.

I defiantly refused to love someone who wasn't, first, my friend. And by the time we were friends, it seemed too late for romance.

> *To the dread of freedom is added the dread of guilt.*
> Madonna Kolbenschlag
> *KISS SLEEPING
> BEAUTY GOOD-BYE*

I and others like me graduated from college doubly burdened—by the past and by the future. Having been kissed by the cold lips of failure (we had found no ready-made home), we looked toward the future with fear that it would return and kiss us—or worse—again.

Until recent years Catholic women in this situation saw convents as the home of tomorrow, as the outlet for service in return for care and lodging. Many Protestant women went to the mission field, or simply went back to their parents' home and waited for the time when homes of their own sprouted roots.

Many women who succeeded, who married right out of college, now look back from middle age. Why did they marry? For love, of course. But also, they say, out of fear. Going out on their own seemed a death at the teeth of sharks; going back home seemed a death by suffocation.

A man stood before a woman, offering, inside a diamond ring, the comfort of a place where she was needed and wanted and the promise of the fulfillment of motherhood.

Did a nervous stomach remind her of her vulnerability, of her position as a model or actress waiting in the lineup of not-impossible-she's who would mother his, someone else's, or no one's children? If she had been chosen once, might she never be chosen again? Did she fear that Solomon might have been right in saying that a barren womb, like the grave and like fire, is never satisfied?

She fell in love. The boundaries of her young, not-well-defined self moved and engulfed some other. She became we and she married.

If she learned to work hard at loving, even after the boundaries of self have lost their emotional elasticity, she is still happy in her choice. If she learned to look hard at who she is and, with the support of the man she loves, found out who she is apart from him, she of all women is fortunate. I wish that all women had the inner assurance of knowing that they had sometime faced their fear of making it on their own, and won their battle over it, freely choosing their course. For those who truly love are "quite capable of living without each other" (M. Scott Peck, *The Road Less Traveled*). Those who have never faced the **fear** are never quite sure whether or not it is as harmless as a blue "cookie monster" or a fiery, charring dragon as fierce as Tolkien's Smaug.

I had heard it before in some psychology class, but it had never sunk in. Now when the entire Sunday sermon centered on it I sat up and took note. It was so obvious, why hadn't I ever taken its application into my working consciousness:

What you fear controls you. What you most fear binds you most tightly.

As much as I feared the freedom of college commencement, I trembled more at the thought of returning to a life that was known and predictable and without choice.

On my graduation afternoon I drove to my parents' home and repacked my car, since the next morning I was to drive two hundred and fifty miles. Destination—a job in publishing. It would pay my bills. It would, I hoped, not be boring. A new city and a job dealing with print and words dangled in front of me the potential of meeting new people and uncovering new ideas.

I knew the unroutinely routine of my parents' lives as well as I knew the alphabet. Having been a part of it once-removed for four years I saw that it indeed did run smoothly without me, and, if I thought about it, I knew that I adequately survived when I was not with them. We were mentally in different worlds. Although I did not know who I was, I knew I was not a carbon copy of either of them. I then thought I was not even a compilation of the two, except in a physical manner. If I stayed geographically close I would be pressed down with expectations not unsimilar to those I felt as a child: Do as we want you to do. Talk as we want you to talk. Become what we want you to become.

I *could* stay if I wanted—they had made that clear, but in no way had they made demands. I knew staying near home would be safe. Although I would have to pay room and board, I would not have to create my own world. I again had to choose—emotional infancy or life separate from them. If I lived near home I would constantly have to fight the magnetic pull back toward the too comfortable world of childhood, when Mother's arms calmed my fears and when Father's judgment was mine. No. I would leave home for real.

I would go look for air to breathe that would be my own.

If we could first know where we were and whither we are tending, we could better judge what to do and how to do it.

Abraham Lincoln

Late that afternoon—of my college graduation—I walked into my parents' bedroom. Their wedding portrait stood on top of the chest of drawers. It had been there for years; I had overlooked it many times, but today it caught my eye. They had married on the afternoon of their college graduation.

For several years I had maintained that I would wear my mother's wedding gown as mine.

I took a break from my packing and asked Mother if I could try on the dress, as I had once before. She pulled the worn box down from the top closet shelf. I unfolded the organdy dress carefully, lest the least bit of pressure cause the material to tear. I held the shoulders up to mine, but gravity had little effect on the wrinkles.

I put it on over my head. My mother, who now wore a size twice mine, had once fitted into this dress which snuggled my hips.

I looked again at the familiar wedding picture. Her graduation day had commenced a new life for her. For her, and then, it was the right choice. Her alternative, late in the Depression, was to go care for her sister's children. She loved Father. She wanted children of her own. Teaching jobs weren't to be found.

She didn't smile for her wedding pose. She looked straight into the camera.

Was she frightened? If she had known then what these thirty-five years and the years still to come would bring her, would she have said, "I do"? If she had known she would birth nine babies, bury two children and pray a third back from the brink of death, would she have bought this dress?

I daresay she would have. I walked from her room into mine. I sat on my bed and stared at myself in my vanity mirror. I wasn't marrying. Today the walk from her room into mine was as far as I would wear this dress. Assuredly, someday I would wear it for the real thing. But now it was simply my reminder. I was not she. She had chosen the obvious path. In that regard we were alike. Leaving seemed the only decision that made any sense for me.

But I was commencing life alone and she had been hand in hand with someone stronger than she. Her affections overwhelmed any fear, whereas I felt my fear of boredom and anonymity driving me toward a fearsome, haunted, lonely faraway castle of dreams where I could discover that I was someone other than my parents' daughter.

I took off Mother's dress and pushed it back into the box. I put the box on the shelf myself and then covered it with stacks of shoe and hat boxes which kept the top of it from getting dusty.

I went back into my room, closed the door, and cried over my union with life.

Mary Ellen left college and moved four hundred miles from her parents' home. She rented an apartment with her college roommate and they both hit the streets looking for work. Her parents had not wanted her to go so far away. They didn't like her going before she had the promise of employment. She was the child of their old age, their only hope for security. They had raised her so that she would help them, and now she was abandoning their choice of life in a small town for the excitement of city living.

Before Mary Ellen boarded the Greyhound bus that would take her away, her mother, teary-eyed, reminded her of her heritage. "When you were just a baby, the WCTU came to the house and claimed you as one of theirs. They tied a white ribbon around your wrist as a symbol of their faith in your growing up and remaining free from the curse of alcohol."

Mary Ellen was a conscientious, dedicated Christian, old enough to be the mother of a kindergartner, struggling with what she was going to do with her life, and her mother was worried that Mary Ellen would forget the past. She was concerned that she had mothered in vain. Mother, fearful of losing daughter, made Mary Ellen's leaving more difficult. The daughter, needing assurance that her mother was still present in her life, needed a parent who assured her that she could make it, needed a parent who had taken Dietrich Bonhoeffer's words to heart: "From the moment we awake until we fall asleep we must commend our loved ones wholly and unreservedly to God and leave them in his hands, transforming our anxiety for them into prayers on their behalf" (Letters and Papers from Prison).

The months would prove that her mother had not, in spirit, lost a daughter. Phone calls came often. Mary Ellen called home after her first grocery shopping trip. The ham she had bought had a moldy rind and the butcher had told her hams always did. Was he taking advantage of her ignorance?

Mary Ellen's mother gave free advice and called back the next day to hear the end of the ham story. Was everything OK?

Yes, yes . . . until the next new domestic experience raised its head, and then her mother was called again.

When Cindy left the Midwest for the East Coast after college graduation, she felt silent, subtle pressure from her father; he didn't want her to leave. He withdrew from her and didn't participate in the family leave-taking. After she left, it was quite some time before he spoke with her on the phone.

They never discussed what he was feeling or why. Only later, when she read *When the Road Bends*, by Karl A. Olsson, did she pinpoint what her father's feelings might have been: "Those who remain [behind when someone moves away] may experience feelings stronger than grief—envy, rejection, hopelessness."

After the fact, young women who leave home are able to put themselves in their parents' place and see the vacuum in the lives of those left behind. Judy felt certain that her mother, who lived in a small Midwestern town, lived vicariously through the life of her daughter. "When I would vacation in the Bahamas, it was as if she were finally having the opportunity to travel. She would want to know all the details of my trip. If I didn't fill my parents in on what I was doing, they made me feel guilty for withholding some part of me that they felt they deserved to have.

"So, in one sense I had left, but in another sense there was still this tug of expectations that verbally drew me back to them. I told them the details that distance had stolen from them."

Nancy called one Sunday afternoon to tell me she had discovered the factor that made this mass exodus of young single women from home possible: the telephone. Her phone had been out of order for forty-eight hours—and on a weekend. She lived alone and was nearly beside herself in her isolation. The first evening, "I paced like a lion in a cage from one room of my apartment to another. I must have picked up the phone twenty times, intently listening for the dial tone that had vanished, thinking maybe its disappearance had been a fleeting, fickle matter. It wasn't. It was as dead as the black plastic itself.

"I couldn't call friends who lived several miles away and ask them to come over for the evening. I couldn't even get rid of the uneasiness by telling someone else about it. I always felt a great comfort in knowing that my parents were on the other end of the phone line—even though halfway across the country. Sometimes I pictured in my mind the network of wires strung from this receiver that was touching my ear to the one that was touching one of their ears.

"I panicked when I didn't have the security of knowing that I could, if I wanted, be talking with any number of close, long-distance friends and relatives. All of a sudden I wanted to talk with all of them at once."

Nancy finally got to the point of her call to me. "So after two days of this restlessness, I saw that I never would have been strong enough to leave home if no magic machine had assured me that I could, at any time, tell them that I was either feeling OK or doing terribly—if there had been no means of instant feedback."

And the same might be said of fast transit. Anyone can get almost anywhere in the States in twenty-four hours. Farewells, as hard as they may be, are rarely permanent. Americans no longer board a covered wagon on the East Coast with the knowledge that, barring a miracle, they will never again see the parents they are leaving behind. Americans are no longer notified of the death of a close family member weeks or even months after the interment. Weddings and funerals may be missed because of lack of funds, but they no longer go unattended because of the physical barrier caused by the combination of distance and time.

Technology has made moving away from home look easier

and less risky than it did in the past. But in their sleepless morning hours, many who have set out on the venture fear where they might be if the technological scaffolding were pulled out from under them.

TWO

AWAY FROM HOME

ALONE

Who defines the rose never seen—
the mutant whose petals
are purple in hue,
who lives a whole season,
from summer through autumn
when death takes its toll
with the freezing of dew?

For the thing which I greatly feared is come upon me.
JOB 3:25

When I pray for you in this new venture, God gives me a good verse: "For God did not give us a spirit of timidity but a spirit of power and of love and self-control" (2 Tim. 1:7). I know that new situations are always fearful, but God's Spirit will be with you.
   We all love you. I will try to not interfere in this new phase of your life when for the first time you are truly on your own, but if you need help anytime of any kind, feel free to ask it.

*Letter from a father to his
daughter upon her moving
into her first apartment,
out of town*

I unloaded my car two hundred and fifty miles away from where Father and I had packed every available inch of its space. I had it planned this way. "I will not own more than I can fit in my car. If 'something happens' and I want to get away fast, I'll not have to worry about leaving anything behind."

Father had prayed nearly the same tearful prayer of good-bye he had said the day I went to college as a freshman, adding a pep talk about how he "knew I could do it."

Of course I would not forget what my parents had taught me; sometimes it frightened me that I seemed to be able to remember nothing else.

I walked to the desk of the White Plains YWCA. Yes, the room they had assured would be mine was ready. I filled the room with stuffed boxes that were secondhand from the grocery store, made my bed, and tried to fall asleep.

Why was this day's move any different from the one four years ago? This room didn't look all that much different from one in a college dormitory. I could still leave in the amount of time it would take me to pack my car.

Yet it seemed so final.

Carol left home in late August. She loaded her car, said good-bye, and promised that she would call back twice on her solo five-hundred-mile maiden voyage to Rochester, New York, where she had accepted a teaching job. On the second call home her father asked her to call again when she reached Rochester. She walked into her apartment, which she was sharing with two other women, and phoned her dad.

"I'm here," she said. "And everything is fine."

"Great," he said, and after he had asked every detail of her trip, he concluded, "Now, Carol, this is the last call for which I will accept the charges. We love you, but you're on your own."

I arranged the furniture. On the wall I hung posters and postcards that connected me to college friends and distant relatives and near memories. I hoped a time would come when I wouldn't miss them, because, whether they were present or not, I would feel the assurance of their long-distance love.

I faced the strangers at the office with a strong-willed, yet restrained determination: "If this is what I have to spend my life doing—basically secretarial work—if this is where I have to be, then rest assured I will do it well and no one will stop me."

My parents, having "adopted" many single graduate students in the past, earnestly prayed that I would find someone who would "take me in," invite me home for Sunday dinner, let me put my shoeless feet on their furniture. Someone who would take my car to the repair shop and who would recommend to me a good inexpensive dentist. I discovered that co-workers were full of advice, but none offered a footstool that was quite as comfortable as the one in my parents' home.

I drove home as often as I could afford—once every month or six weeks (more often, it seemed, than I had gone home from college). Driving through the Catskills, which in May had caused visions of my car plunging over the guardrails and down the side of a mountain, grew to be a leisurely trip.

In the winter I would start the journey even when the weatherman predicted conditions that would now keep me housebound. My youth threw caution to the wind.

As in college days, I took laundry home to wash in Mother's machine. I took the car home for Father to maintain. Although New York City stores were at my fingertips, I shopped in the small suburban mall near my parents' home.

It was always hard for me to account for how I had spent my hours while at their house. The two or three days would end and I had done very little. I puttered near Mother in the kitchen although she did most of the work. Occasionally I would sew a skirt in the dining room while Mother would talk to me from the kitchen, or occasionally I would wash my car. But mostly I would "unwind," as Mother called it; I would walk around the house, soaking up the familiar. Tensions, like dry skin, would flake off and strength, like hand lotion, would seep in.

These visits, although refreshing, were never as good as I had envisioned they would be. Jean, recently out of graduate school and away from home, also encountered this letdown—her anticipation exceeding the reality of the visit. She had always planned these great conversations she was going to have with her mother while home, but when she saw her mother face-to-face the plans for talking woman-to-woman disintegrated. They fell into old, outdated (yet familiar) models of communicating.

> *In anticipation of a visit with her [my daughter], I would save up scraps of conversational material for us to share, amusing and revealing bits and pieces that would surely patch over the gaping holes of time and space that separated us. This time, I would tell myself, we will find out who we really are, how we think, how we have changed in these last years—and we'll draw together and enjoy each other as we used to. But somehow we would never have these talks. When the moment came, my courage would fail me, and I would remain within the familiar and protective shelter of Parenthood.*
>
> Elinor Lenz
> *ONCE MY CHILD . . .*
> *NOW MY FRIEND*

Sensing that my separation from my parents was wide, whether I was with them or far from them, made me depressed. They were not the "pals" I made them out to be when I was far away and in a situation where everyone I met was a stranger. Yet their presence alone gave me a comfort I wished I could lean on all the time.

Leaving their home on Sunday afternoon to make the return trip was, without question, traumatic. An observer would have thought I was planning never to return. That was not the point; I was leaving the comfort of being known (at least in the past tense) by those whom I knew, and heading into a living and work situation where I felt my every action was under the scrutiny of judging eyes.

Will we get along? Will we tolerate each other? Or will we lock horns? were the questions I mentally asked of everyone I met, and the same questions they asked of me.

Would this new acquaintance prove to be a good friend? Someone I would trust or someone with whom I must feel guarded? I was joining already established circles of friends.

At work, which kaffeeklatsch should I join? There were, I noticed, distinct separations. On the job, would I meet the expected standards? I knew this nine-to-five world was different from the more objective and more casual college scene. If a supervisor took an aversion toward the way you organized your desk, you could be suspect. I was not one of many new college students simultaneously starting out a fresh year; I was one new bottom-rung employee walking into an office full of seasoned "old-timers" who knew that I could easily be replaced. They were paying me; I was not, as in college, paying them.

> *Because I was unhappy and rejoiced in my unhappiness, I felt harsh. Because I was hurt at being torn from my . . . baby brother, I had to turn away from home and faith and all the gentle things of life and seek the hard.*
>
> Dorothy Day
> THE LONG
> LONELINESS

Except behind the locked door of my small YWCA room that did not in the least seem truly mine, White Plains, New York—my Sunday afternoon destination—provided no corner in which I felt safe. Like a soldier girding up his loins for battle, I bolstered myself with fresh courage and drove from my parents' house to my room—down the now familiar highway, toward my "Gettysburg," my live-or-die turning point.

Again, why didn't I just say, "I'm not going to White Plains; I'm staying here, basking in the comfort"? Mother especially would have been delighted if I had then made that choice. On Sunday afternoons she often asked me that exact question. I'm not sure why I didn't. I somehow felt that if I stayed, it would still be on my parents' terms. I still didn't know enough about myself to return home and continue to hold my own. For me, returning would still have meant becoming a shadow of a previous generation—maybe a frightening, ghostly shadow.

Moving closer to home has been the answer for some young women. Some have returned home out of monetary necessity—their entry-level salaries could not sustain their independent life-styles. Others have returned for emotional support. Most agree that actually moving back into the same household as their parents' is extremely difficult.

For a short while Nancy went back home to live. She would be with people to whom she was important. Her parents would provide her with a roof and therefore some of her responsibility would be eased. She wrote a letter: "Mom doesn't like me around . . . unless I will fall into the pattern of her playing the little girl's mama, which I am not, nor is she. She gets really cross when I mention my having to leave soon. Makes me feel like a traitor or deserter because I'm trying to get a job and get off their backs. So, you just can't win—when away from home you miss it, when at home you can't live there like you once did."

Or maybe the problem is that it is all too much like it once was. If the roles of childhood days have not been broken and remolded in an adult fashion before the return move, conflict is inevitable. And even so, you are moving back into *their* house, in which they have established the house rules, staked out the territories, chosen the furniture, paid most of the mortgage, and so forth.

Jean also saw the problem: "When I go home, I melt into their pot. We spend time doing what Mother wants to do, which usually means we go shopping, even when I don't want to or need to shop. They are the leaders; I am the follower.

"I could go back home, but that is the price I'd have to pay. I just guess it's true that 'you can't go home again.'" Not, anyway, when you grew up having the assumption that you would someday leave the nest so you could go and build one of your own.

I only tolerated the YWCA, yet stayed a whole year thinking I could afford nothing better, although I never actually looked to see what the going prices were. Even apartment *hunting* sounded too permanent. It probably would mean signing a year's lease. I didn't give much thought to a year away; when I did it was never in the context of still having the same job, being in the same city, or, heaven forbid, living alone.

A YWCA, although transient in nature, resembled the familiarity of a college dorm. Its communal type of living at least provided people who ate dinner across the table from me, help in case of sickness, and laughter at an occasional joke.

But a home? Hardly. I was in my room as little as possible. Every week brought the same question: What will be this weekend's diversion? I did not *want* the room to be my place of rest. There was nothing about secretarial work, a YWCA, or White Plains, New York, that I hoped would become a part of who I was. Again, or still, an ambivalence tore at my center. I craved permanence but wasn't willing to step toward making what I had seen even temporarily permanent.

A year dragged into two. Through a conversation with a co-worker, I "accidentally" stumbled upon a tiny furnished apartment, for which the landlord did not want a lease. There was no oven. Through the walls I could hear the landlord belch his beer. If the refrigerator came on while I was cooking on the hot plate, a fuse blew. But at least I had my own telephone and my own bathroom. It made life more comfortable; it gave a semblance of having a place of my own, yet the freedom of still being able to leave it all on short notice.

During their first independent years, many women can deal with little more than their decisions to leave home in pursuit of their own niche. Carrying out that one decision, putting one foot in front of the other to get through the day, consumes their energies. Deciding what, if anything, to cook for dinner is a production.

They want a mother or a "wife" who will take care of the humdrum of life—the shopping, the cooking, balancing the checkbook. Such chores make one so connected to the present that it demands that one touch it, hear it, smell it, see it, and taste it. They make running from it into some imaginary other-than-here, past or future, impossible.

But exactly what is the future they imagine themselves a part of? For some it changes from one minute to the next; it is just *not* what has proved to be the here and now. Sometimes they see themselves in some position of power. In charge. At their word, people jump. Sometimes they are romping, carefree, in a never-ending field of clover. Sometimes they are cooking dinner for someone else. Sometimes they are accusing no one in particular of having lied to them; why hadn't someone told them how difficult it was really going to be. They had been brought up to love, not to live.

It never once crossed my mind that no one had told me what life as an independent woman would be like because relatively few women older than I had truly walked through this doorway. They hadn't chosen this alternative. I think of my father's family. All of his sisters, married or single, had settled within forty miles of their parents' farm. My cousins were following the same pattern.

It was truly the exception for a woman to go off on her own to seek her fortune or home. She waited, in familiar environs, until they came to her. At least, while waiting for the future, she was consoled by her continuity with her past.

I had seen only a few glimpses into the lives of women who had attempted what I was in the midst of. One woman, fifteen years my senior, told me over coffee in her small-town Pennsylvania home that she had tried the independent career route for about six months when she was just out of college.

"I couldn't do it," she said. "I did what I had to do to find a husband. When I married him the issue wasn't love, it was survival."

Should I give up, I wondered, and marry anyone I could find? Should I give up and go back home, or should I stick it out one more month?

There would be days in the next five years when I would call my older brother and announce that tomorrow I was going to quit work.

"Why tomorrow?" he would ask.

"Because I can't take it anymore. I've just got to get out of here."

He would always say the same thing. "Well, you'd have to give two weeks' notice, right?"

Of course he was right.

"So, you have no choice but to stay that long. Why don't

you not say anything for two weeks, and then if you still feel as strongly convinced that you must leave as you do now, go ahead. Resign."

Resign to go where?

I picked a city. The city where I had grown up, from which we had moved when I was a young teenager, was my hideaway. The passing of years had caused a heavenly glow to fall in my mind over that city. If I went there everything would work out. I would find employment, be within two hours of my parents' home and within several hours of most of my siblings.

But I never did make the move. Two weeks later I never felt quite so convinced that returning was the answer I needed. Along with my college roommate, Suzanne, who was now in a similar situation, I feared: "I keep getting these horrible premonitions that things won't change, even if I do change places. I try not to think of that too much."

I attempted again to fill the hours. Talking to myself was not enough to assure me of my existence or my necessity or my relevance to the world beyond myself.

The telephone, I knew, was the answer, the instrument that would define me. If I could convince myself that someone was thinking of me, right now and in the present, I found it easier to think of myself in terms of the now and in terms of this current pleasant conversation. A roommate was not now feasible or desirable; the telephone was the next best thing to old friends being with me in person. When they were listening to me or I to them, they had little choice but to be reminded that I was alive and well. They connected me to the me they knew, the me I had been, the me that existed despite the fact that I did not know who the me was that I wanted to become.

You can't appreciate home till you've left it.

O. Henry
*THE FOURTH IN
SALVADOR*

Sally, after college and her first job, moved from her native state to Oklahoma—looking for a home of her own that was affordable. Her mother flew out for a visit, and one evening happened to walk into Sally's bedroom while Sally was there drying her hair. Something snapped. Sally burst into tears and fell into her mother's arms, sobbing. "I could die and no one would know it."

"The feeling was horrible, so consuming," she told me later. "But I didn't for a minute think about moving back home. I couldn't; I was an adult."

> *It was a beginning, I remembered. Filing, typing, making coffee—and learning everything I could about broadcasting. . . . I wanted a career. I was young, I had potential, I felt full of hope for the future and not at all homesick. If anyone had said to me then that twenty years later a therapist would tell me to give up my dependence on my parents, I wouldn't have believed it. I felt truly liberated. I had cut the cord and was happy to be on my own.*
>
> Barbara Gordon
> *I'M DANCING AS FAST*
> *AS I CAN*

After a week of intense abdominal pain, I surrendered myself to the emergency room doctors. When I could no longer stand up straight, I knew I could no longer hide out. Even so, I was confident that they would find nothing wrong and release me after their reconnaissance.

Wrong. Infection strictly confined me to a half-inclined hospital bed for one week.

I was visiting friends in Boston (one of my many attempts at escaping for the weekend). I desperately wanted the doctors to "give me something" so I could get back to New York and take care of it there. "You, young lady, are going nowhere," was their firm verdict.

My hostess and host were marvelous. They drove me to the hospital at three in the morning. They stayed with me, as much as doctors allowed, in the examining room. They made inane middle-of-the-night jokes that kept my mind off the pain, except that it hurt so much to laugh. They saw me to my permanent room, and to rest. I was grateful for their care, but . . .

But I wanted my mother.

I was twenty-four, too old for this kind of infantile desire. I now wonder if I hadn't been slowly pushing myself toward the brink of total physical collapse, waiting for someone to come and pick up the pieces.

Yes, she said she would come. What she was supposed to do for me, I didn't know. I would still have to deal with the early-morning doctor visit. Her presence would not convince anyone to let me out of bed any earlier than the next Saturday. Yet my pain started to lift the minute I knew the plane she had boarded was in the air. And in that moment I quit fighting. I willingly allowed myself the luxury of being chained by intravenous tubes to my sickbed. I was not responsible for my work, for my transportation, even for taking care of myself.

For three days Mother spent every minute of every visiting hour at my side. And I reveled in her healing power, transmitted to my body and spirit by osmosis. But Wednesday came quickly. Father awaited her back home, and she intended to keep her return plane reservation. Although thankful for the "vacation," I knew things must return to normal.

Once again I tearfully mourned her departure and the passing of time—the cause of what then seemed our eternal separation. I knew I must draw my strength from God, my ultimate source of breath and hope.

It had happened before, this parental plucking from the flames of fire. Many times I suppose, but none quite so dramatic as the ordeal of second-grade gym class. A portion of that year's physical education program was spent on "tumbling and gymnastics." About all I could manage was a basic forward and backward roll. If a spotter was doing all the work, I could pretend that I was standing on my head or successfully completing a backward flip. But the two ropes that dangled from the ceiling might as well have been installed for the purpose of hanging innocent eight-year-old girls. As hard as I tugged, I could not pull my weight off the knot tied at the bottom of the hemp snake. I heard the teacher's "Try again" as "You must, or else . . ." although I didn't know what was at the end of the sentence other than possibly a failing mark, which, for the grade's star pupil was a brand worse that Hester's scarlet A.

It was not a schemed plot, but nausea systematically attacked early every Tuesday and Thursday morning. The first and second days this happened I was allowed to stay home. But the next week, I was pushed, in tears, out the front door. One of these mornings I remember standing on the large hot-air register in the living room. I was sharing its heat with my father's legs, holding on to them as if they were pillars of the earth itself. "Why don't you want to go to school?" he asked.

I hadn't told him I didn't want to go to school. That wasn't the problem. The problem was that I was going to throw up.

"What happens on Tuesdays that you don't like?"

Well, if he phrased the question that way, the answer was "Gym class."

"And what about gym class?"

"I'm just not strong enough."

He laid his hands on my shoulders and told me that I had to get on the school bus, that I had to go to gym class, that I had to try as hard as I could to do what they expected of me, but if pulling as hard as I could didn't do the trick, I should not be ashamed of myself or afraid of the consequences.

I boarded the bus, and two hours later was summoned into the principal's office. He told me that I should sit on his secretary's lap. And he told me to tell them what was upsetting me so much. The same story. But I wondered how he knew about my upset stomach.

Later that week I was called to the gym teacher's office. "You know I'm only asking you to do your best."

No, I didn't know, but it was sinking in, and so was the fact that Father had intervened. In calling the school, he had removed the stinger from the bee whose poison was deadly, considering the smallness of my girl-sized frame.

For the remainder of the gymnastics term my arms strained to pull my head up to my hands. All attempts failed, but I remained satisfied with having done my best.

"No matter how strong we are, no matter how caring and responsible and adult, if we look clearly into ourselves we will find the wish to be taken care of for a change. Each one of us, no matter how old and mature, looks for and would like to have in his or her life a satisfying mother figure and father figure" (M. Scott Peck, *The Road Less Traveled*). Dr. Peck goes on to say that the lives of healthy people are not dictated by these feelings.

Easy for a man to say, I thought. They're programmed to let go.

The introductory movie, explaining the life and politics of colonial Williamsburg, Virginia, just prior to the outbreak of the Revolution, was nearing its end. Samuel Frye, a patriot on whose life the film centered, had to decide—would he or would he not vote for Virginia's independence? The very same morning his son had to decide—would he or would he not answer the roll call of the colonial militia? Both decided they would gamble their lives and fortunes for the cause of freedom; they would do what had to be done.

Father and son shared intense "God be with you" farewells and best wishes. They went their separate manly ways, with heads held high and eyes bright and firm.

And where is Mr. Frye's daughter? I asked myself.

Far away at the estate house waiting for some soldier home from the war to take her from her father's roof and her mother's arms, under and into his.

It all seemed so healthy two hundreds years ago, and seems so convenient now—until age, death, or divorce dissolves the protecting shingles. The rain that then falls is capable of immobilizing.

Mary, age twenty-eight, found herself in the throes of a split between herself and her boyfriend. On several different nights she woke at 3:00 A.M. from a fitful sleep, crying for her mother. But Mary was in California and her mother in Virginia. The possibility of her mother heeding her call was out of the question.

If Mary had been dying her mother would have come, but

heartbreaks were not seen as life-or-death emergencies. Mary knew that if Mother were really the cure-all for her misery, she herself would have boarded a plane to Virginia and stayed there until all was healed. But the yearning, which was verbalized as a need for Mother, was for something larger than Mother. What force held and comforted a woman as a mother did a child? A man, yes, but he was gone and that was the problem.

She grieved his loss by crying for one who would gather her under warm wings as a hen gathers her chicks.

But the intensity of her struggle waned, and within a few days life was again before her, demanding her response.

The storms come and then go. And as Elisabeth Elliot might say, they must be endured.

Events that a few years ago kept me totally preoccupied have now become vague memories; conflicts that a few months ago seemed so crucial in my life now seem futile and hardly worth the energy; inner turmoil that robbed me of my sleep only a few weeks ago has now become a strange emotion of the past; books that filled me with amazement a few days ago now do not seem as important; thoughts which kept my mind captive only a few hours ago, have not lost their power and have been replaced by others.
Henri J. M. Nouwen
A CRY FOR MERCY

And so, the first years of independence move on.

Was I the only one who spent every waking hour of twenty-five years waiting for the day when I-knew-not-quite-what would happen? The older I grew, the more undefined the soon-to-arrive event was, but the more convinced I became that I would know it when I saw it. Something, the likes of which I'd never experienced, would whisk me, the child always preparing for the future, into the very center point of that future. From there, I knew I would be able to look out and, in every direction, see the world, my world,

*spinning around me instead of looking at it through a
fogged-over crystal ball. And the day that would
happen, the purpose of my existence would be made
clear; my existence would somehow be justified. . . .*

*Those next five years, I think, were spent waiting
for the return of the first twenty when at least I knew
with great certainty that eventually something good
was going to happen to me.*

> Twenty-five-year-old single
> career woman

After one and a half years of typing purchase orders and
answering the telephone, I was bored. I couldn't see this as
my life spread before me. In my journal I wrote, "This can't
be it. Life begins next Tuesday," in much the same vein as
Emily Dickinson's lines:

> And life is over there
> Behind the shelf
> The sexton keeps the key to.

"What are you going to be when you grow up?" one twenty-
five-year-old secretary asked another. The question had just
slipped out, without real thought of what she was implying.
There was a long pause. The two women looked each other in
the eye and then both burst out laughing.

"Well, if I'm not going to have babies, I sure don't want to
be a clerk/typist the rest of my life." Even the answer had
"just slipped out."

Some kind of trade-off existed in her mind, as if having a
husband or babies would make this kind of nine-to-five living excusable or even enjoyable. She had to be able to define
herself in a role that was respectable in someone else's eyes.
If she were married and mothering children, the women's
magazines, the church, her husband, and her children themselves would tell her that she had done the right thing, made
the right choice. If she were on her way up a corporate
ladder, she would be able to say that she was progressing,
proceeding as one would expect of an ambitious, career-
minded person. She didn't let herself think about the fact

that she felt she had to succeed in either the traditional male role or the traditional female role. She hoped, of course, that she might be able to juggle success in both worlds, but feared she might not succeed in either.

Could she give herself completely to this career climb (it might mean changing companies or relocating to a new city) when half of her knew that, more than this, she eventually wanted babies of her own? What if gambling careerwise precluded marriage? What if "men don't like women who know too much" proved to be true? In ten years, would she regret her current decision?

With the exception of women who have already made life-long commitments to a religious order, I have not found even one female never-been-married Christian under thirty-five who says she would not like to be married ten years from now. Either the dread of aloneness or the dream of building a home like their parents had, or like they wish their parents could have had, pushes them to look ahead toward the life they hope to have in the future. Like Laura, in Tennessee Williams' *The Glass Menagerie*, they yearn for the "long delayed but always expected something" that will bring life.

Dealing with the present as if it might be permanent is rarely considered—especially when nine-to-five is less than the ultimate ideal.

For many women, work must either be stimulating or must be put up with for the benefit of someone other than self. "I could do this rather mindless work for the rest of my life if I were doing it so that someone I loved, and someone who appreciated it, could eat better or live more fully," commented one woman who found her work boring. One must either love to work or work for love, it seems. Or, as another woman commented, "The world is full of cookees and cookers. It doesn't seem fair that I should have to be both people wrapped into one."

There is a certain kind of impersonality which kills a woman's interest. If her work is purely mechanical, such as filing index cards, or moving a lever to and fro on a machine, her interest is, as a rule, not satisfied, as a man's perhaps might be, in working out a new system, or in discovering how it is done, or even in coming to love the machine. She will either become a sort of robot or she will turn away from the task and occupy herself with the person for whom she is doing it.

But a personal motive will carry a woman through an almost unlimited amount of monotonous work without the risk of losing her soul.

Esther Harding
THE WAY OF ALL WOMEN

Sometimes working for the sake of putting food on your own plate hardly seems incentive enough. Without someone to cook for and eat with, eating barely seems necessary.

"Sometimes I can't remember whether I've eaten or not," one woman said. "Or I can remember that I've eaten, but I don't get any satisfaction from it. I feel just as hungry, or just as not hungry before eating as after eating. I do it only because I know that if I don't, I'll eventually get sick."

She says it sometimes comes down to playing games with herself, talking herself into "I deserve a well-cooked meal," and then puttering in the kitchen until she comes up with it.

When I started thinking about the present as possibly being permanent I would get sorely depressed. I saw sixty-year-old women who were still typing letters. They had been doing it for forty years. They were proof to me that family life was not inevitable. They were sour, bitter women who felt that life had dealt them a bad hand. Was there a cause-and-effect relationship in their circumstances? Were they bitter because they were alone and in less than responsible positions, or were they alone and in these positions because they had been melancholic to begin with? Whichever the case, I feared it was the first, and if it happened to them, it could happen to me. This could go on forever.

Ministers who talked of living victoriously by depending on Jesus made me walk away in disgust. Sure they depended on Jesus, but I doubted that they depended on him any more than on their wives and the security which that relationship brought them. I felt some satisfaction when one such minister admitted that, if he had a job he hated and no wife and children to lean on, he would probably be an alcoholic. Now there, I thought, is someone who understands himself.

Friends in situations similar to mine wrote me letters. They were starting to hate themselves for the amount of time they spent daydreaming, building for themselves a world in which they were indispensable. Sometimes it was a rerun of childhood's happier days, sometimes it was what they wished the present or the future would hold.

What could I do to get myself out of this trap? I didn't know, but for a diversion I started playing solitaire. A journal entry from that time reads: "I spend hours playing solitaire, pretending that maybe while I'm playing, the phone will ring. But it doesn't. And I don't feel better after I've won. So evenings fly by and I'm waiting, waiting . . . for who knows what."

I wasn't alone in thinking this was an answer. In *A Different Woman*, author Jane Howard's sister, Ann, notes: "Solitaire may be the secret underground vice of American womanhood. I have more friends than you might think who say, 'Well, I think I'll just flip through this deck one more time.'" But one more time never brought more fulfillment than did the last time through.

Doras, instinctively knowing that food has or should have some magic life-giving quality, waited—for her career to open up or for a compatible, permanently present man to appear—by overeating. One more bowlful, like one more game, distracted her from the reality of the present, and from the fear that this might be the future her parents had always been preparing her for.

"I feel wasted," wrote Nancy. Her education had taught her how to think; it had promised her a place worthy of notice, but doors had not opened. She was basically alone, and she was impatient. She waited in her entry-level position for the right nod from the right person.

A career, so it seemed, took time to build. Youth, especially female youth, were supposed to stand the test of time, and then, and only maybe, they would be rewarded with more responsibility. But as much as we coveted the responsibility, its countenance looked frightening.

What if I liked it? What if I loved it enough that I would never want to give it up? What if I stuck my neck out and said, "Yes. I have decided. I'm going to be _____, something. I'm going to make a name for myself and love every minute of it"?

But it seemed terribly unchristian, or at least unfeminine. I was not to want authority or power. It puzzled me that most of the Christian men I spoke with never interpreted Jesus' teachings in that manner, but many women I knew felt the conflict strongly. One woman recently commented, "As I gained professional confidence, I lost some of my confidence as a Christian." I was supposed to want to be a servant, a lowly helper. I did want to be a servant, but I also wanted respect, and in the work world, servants received no such thing.

One woman's journal reveals her frustrations: "And even if I wanted to give my life to a career, I couldn't [speaking in the voice of her background]. Because if the chance for marriage and inevitably children came along, my life pursuit would have to change in midstream. My career goals can never be set too strong for fear they will be broken by the call of a homing pigeon. Why must a woman be called to give her all for a man, when a man finds home a place to hang his hat?

"And when a girl is twenty-two and single, and is asked, 'What do you want to do?' why must she give a career goal, when inside she is screaming, 'I want to be a mother,' for to say it makes her some desperate case that embarrasses those already with husband or wife? Society says she must have a lofty goal, yet not take that goal too seriously lest she be asked the golden question—whether she is willing to forsake all for her true love."

At age twenty-nine, Nancy is still floundering from one entry-level position to the next. She's articulate, intelligent, more than capable. She simply has not been in the right place at the right time. She thinks about the future. Even more than when she was twenty-four, she thinks about the fact that things could be this way forever. She has learned that life does not promise a climb up the ladder. She still struggles with the purpose for her world and comments, "Working to sustain my own life hardly seems worthwhile, sometimes."

She keeps looking for her niche. She keeps praying that, if this is where she is to be for an extended period of time, she will learn to be content. But even that, she knows, will take more time.

As is the mother, so is her daughter.
                                        EZEKIEL 16:44

Kathy cringed at hearing her mother's discontented words. She did not want to acknowledge that this part of her mother had become a part of herself. Her mother had sighed and said: "The phone hasn't rung all day. Nobody cares."

Kathy grew angry with her. How could she, who had an ever-present husband, a quiverful of healthy grown children, and a church full of attentive friends, feel forgotten because the bell of the telephone had not rung once in a ten-hour span of daylight?

Kathy wanted to set her mother down and remind her of all the phone calls she had complained of receiving—those that had borne bad news or a responsibility she had felt unprepared to carry. There were days her mother would have given anything for the phone to stop ringing, for helpless or demanding voices to silence their endless talk. But those days—on these days—were forgotten.

"The sins of the mothers" had been visited upon the daughters. Nothing was ever quite good enough for either of them. Kathy could not get away from what she loved or what she hated in her mother.

Virginia Woolf wrote, "We think back through our mothers if we are women" *(A Room of One's Own)*. Simone de Beauvoir noted of her mother, "Our relationship lived on in me in its double-aspect—a subjection that I loved and hated" *(A Very Easy Death)*. Jane Howard said, "In some odd way, I have become her [Mother]" *(Families)*.

Kathy liked to think she was very different from her mother, but sometimes suspected they were frighteningly alike—in their struggles, if not in the working out of them.

Her mother's need for love was as tangible as Kathy's own. They both wanted more than they had. They both thought they deserved more of something. They both saw the answers as being somewhere outside of themselves.

It's not as though I'm climbing a career ladder by leaps and bounds where I am. I'm confused about my future, my desires, my ambitions, my skills.

Cindy, age twenty-four

Is it our [a parent's] very "success" that has bred a generation for whom narcissism may be the only refuge from a competition they are certain they would lose and that they are not at all sure they want to win? . . . "You've let us down" is the silent reproach that speaks to them louder than words. What we often fail to see is how this wedges them into a tight spot, between the rock of our expectations and the hard place of a world of diminishing resources.

Elinor Lenz
ONCE MY CHILD . . .
NOW MY FRIEND

THREE

THE SEARCH FOR RESPECT

BUSINESS TRIP TO CAPE COD

Wet tide-out sand
between sandals and hose
puts long day's work on "hold";
September salt air
brings blood into veins
flushed dry by fierce independence,
and pink western sky
sings the blues to the one
who last month
sold her heart to the corporation.

*I've always wanted my life to be a steady flow, a
continuity. But it seems it's been nothing but stops and
starts, endings and new beginnings.*

Barbara Gordon
I'M DANCING AS FAST AS I CAN

One and a half years went by.
A job in the editorial department opened up. If I asked for it,
the worst they could say would be: "No, you should stay
where you are." If I could somehow get more challenging
tasks, although not necessarily more ultimate responsibility,
I could survive a few more years.

I read, or heard secondhand, of people who woke up, five
days a week, dreading work. I remembered one summer during college when I filed invoices for three months. If there
wasn't enough work to keep me busy, I had to labor at looking feverishly, productively occupied. On those days I truly

despised work. No. It wasn't that I hated what I was doing, it was that I needed the hope of knowing it would soon end.

Like Jane Eyre, who "tired of the routine of eight years in one afternoon," I inwardly wished for a "new servitude." All she wanted was "to serve elsewhere," and she knew that end was not so difficult if she "had only a brain active enough to ferret out the means of attaining it."

Over the course of a Thanksgiving break, which I was spending with my older brother, I had to make this decision which would determine the flow of my future.

Did I see myself as happier in the new job than I currently was? he asked. If I were going to choose to be anywhere or anything, where and what would I be? (I didn't know.) Was the new job taking me in a direction I might like to explore? I wasn't committing myself forever, he tried to assure me. But if I didn't take the next step that, at the time, seemed obvious, I might find myself waiting forever for an escalator magically to place itself under my feet.

My brother thought that God was capable of shutting off the power of the escalator, but he wasn't so sure that God often made a practice of moving entire staircases. I had to choose whether to step or to stand. I had to make a decision.

Carl Jung wrote that masculine decision-making involves "knowing what one wants and doing what is necessary to achieve it" *(Civilization in Transition)*. And in relation to that, his associate, Esther Harding, wrote, "The professional woman . . . is compelled to work directly for what she wants" *(The Way of All Women)*. It was time to step forthrightly in a specific direction. I discovered what Jane Eyre had discovered long before me: "Those who want situations advertise." I did want a new situation. I wanted self-respect and respect from others, which included my family.

At the next family reunion I would have something to say for myself. I had always been able to handle the "When are you going to get married?" question with a short "I haven't had an offer I couldn't refuse." That always brought a laugh and kept people from asking a second question. But I hadn't been able to handle the "What are you doing with yourself?" question without feeling as if I were apologizing for my fruitless existence. If I received the transfer, I would feel that some self-definition was in the early stages of formation.

It was against my reserved nature, but I asked for the switch of departments, and I received the green light. Personnel seemed pleased that I had expressed an interest; they simply hadn't thought of me in terms of that position.

The new challenge frightened me. What if I were found to be capable only of work I thought boring? This was not, after all, the obvious move for someone with a degree in business administration.

I managed. I thrived. A year. A year and a half. I received a raise. They were pleased. At last I could describe who I was in terms of something unique. Not everyone could do what I was doing, whereas I was sure anyone could function at my previous duties. I was one step up the ambitious ladder to success.

I would, I could, prove to my family, to myself, to anyone who cared enough to notice, that I was not a failure at life.

The new job was never quite finished. It was easy to let it consume me. I took it home with me evenings and weekends. The more time I spent on it, the more I accomplished; the more I accomplished, the more positive feedback I received, and then the better I felt about myself.

I was not quite sure if I liked the feedback or if I liked what I was doing. After the newness wore off, there were still days when it was not stimulating, when I didn't quite know who I was or how long I wanted to be there.

I did know one thing: I never regretted having sought out the change.

Lynn couldn't get out of her head one line her father had said to a roomful of people fifteen years before. She had long ago realized that she had personalized a statement she shouldn't have, but she couldn't exorcise it from her brain. Her father put men and women in separate, distinct categories. Not that he was right in thinking that way, but at least she rationally understood his reasoning. His statement had been referring in general to the specific male gender.

Not to her. But her mind didn't separate men from women as clearly as did his. People were people. What was good for Joe should be good for Jane.

If her father were ever to know that his comment had swirled in her mind, like damp laundry in a dryer, for over a decade, he would have been distraught in his remorse. Children should remember only things that will make them grow strong and more able to cope; they should forget the mistakes that cause nightmares—but who's to tell if or when nightmares are looms that weave steel into waking hours.

Lynn's father had just heard of a missionary friend who was giving up his ministry and coming home. The man said he needed more time with his children and so he intended to find a strictly eight-hour-a-day job in construction. The man was a talented, educated mission worker. Lynn's father, a pastor who was consumed with his work, thought the man was wasting God-given talents. The words spilled out: "It's a pity if, when you look back on someone's life, all you can say is that he raised a family."

Lynn took his observation into herself and started thinking about the fact that she had better not be content with just raising children. When she died, she had better have something more to show for her life. She had better be buried with respect.

> It's a thousand pities, Lady, that you weren't a man.
> Bardia, Captain of the
> Guard, to Princess Orual
> C. S. Lewis, TILL WE HAVE FACES

I was home visiting my parents. Sunday morning the telephone rang. My younger brother had been in an accident. The doctors gave little cause for hope.

For two days we sat in vinyl chairs in a hot, enclosed hospital waiting room. I then left, but my parents sat for five more days waiting for life to revive.

That weekend is a blur in my memory. Besides the trauma of the accident, I had that week been given a promotion. This time, I had not asked for it. I felt pride and a sense of accomplishment (although I would have been furious if I had not been given it). But more than the positive emotions, I was again feeling fear. Along with Colette Dowling, I felt that "my conflicting desires to be both free [successful] and safe kept me bound" *(The Cinderella Complex)*. The job was too big. It was a giant and I was a grasshopper in its sight. I was about to be trampled beyond recognition.

I was going back to work on Tuesday, desperately in need of Father's usual "You can conquer the world" prayer-veiled speech, and instead of hearing it I saw my father as a man who hardly had the willpower to get out of a chair. Although he did not verbalize it, I sensed that he had given up. How could God do this to him? He had been faithful. He had already lost two sons to death. Didn't God owe him this son's future?

Where was the parent who, with God, had always chased away the giants or at least given me courage to go fight them off? He didn't look as if he would have won a battle with me, let alone with someone his own size.

Was I going to have to go back to New York and fight this one myself? I remembered the family laughing at a story they loved to tell—of a church Christmas decorating bee from the days before I was born. Father, the pastor, while connecting the star to the top of the twelve-foot tree, fell off the ladder. One of the young boys in the church related with great flourish the story to his mother: "And then God fell down from the top of the tree."

Why had I not learned long ago that Father and God were not one? Intellectually, of course, I knew. I knew that he was not omniscient, but I still somehow clung to the hope that he would always give me tips on how to carry my burdens when they got too heavy for me, just in the same way he gave me tips on how to pack every inch of my car's trunk. No matter how many boxes and bags and suitcases I wanted to get into my car, Father always managed to squeeze them in. I never remembered hearing him say, "There's no more room." There was always another rearrangement that allowed something else to fit.

Sometimes I hated him for too liberally giving advice that was too conservative. I struggled with the guilt I felt if I chose some action other than the one he saw best. But now when I wanted to hear something, and the whole situation seemed beyond his control, I was disheartened. He was not in charge. He sat waiting for the doctors, and ultimately for God, to save him—the part of him that was his son.

So where was I? Alone. Not knowing that my brother would eventually recover, I was letting go of one dear to me, and taking the first job ever given me that involved real responsibility.

I needed reassurance. I needed to know that I could walk without fainting, when I did not have parental words as a crutch on which to lean.

> *"Grandfather!" I cried, no Queen now; all Orual, even all child. "Do they mean you'll leave me? Go away?" . . . And now this game of queenship, which had buoyed me up and kept me busy ever since I woke that morning, failed me utterly.*
>
> The newly hailed Queen
> C. S. Lewis, TILL WE HAVE FACES

> *A mother is not a person to lean on, but a person to make leaning unnecessary.*
>
> Dorothy Canfield Fisher
> HER SON'S WIFE

Several years later I discovered this entry in Oswald Chambers' devotional, *My Utmost for His Highest*, which showed that others before had felt the same struggle when walking alone:

> *"It is not wrong to depend upon Elijah [parent-figure] as long as God gives him to you, but remember the time will come when he will have to go; when he stands no more to you as your guide and leader, because God does not intend he should. You—'I cannot go on without Elijah.' God says you must.*
>
> *". . . You will find yourself at your wits' end and at the beginning of God's wisdom. When you get to your wits' end and feel inclined to succumb to panic, don't. . . . Put into practice what you learned with your Elijah, use his*

*cloak and pray. Determine to trust in God and do not
look for Elijah any more."*

I read one line over and over. "If you remain true to what
you learned with Elijah, you will get the sign that God is
with you."

Upon reading Oswald Chambers, I remembered that I had
received what I felt was a sign that God would see me
through the new job. It had come from the pen of Martin
Luther, from the hymn "A Mighty Fortress Is Our God," and
it was portions of one verse that I repeated when I felt as if I
were drowning:

> Did we in our own strength confide,
> Our striving would be losing;
> Were not the right Man on our side,
> The Man of God's own choosing:
> Dost ask who that may be?
> Christ Jesus, it is He;
> . . . And He must win the battle.

He, not I, not even the part of my parents that was in me,
was my strength. What Father and Mother had taught me
about God I must never forget; but it was God, not a person,
who gave the winning push.

I jumped headlong into the new job. I was always amazed
that other people perceived me as being much more in control of things than I myself did. The days ran smoothly; the
nights, when I crashed from striving so intently for eight
hours, were all a blur. In a year's time, I knew it would be
easy to stay here in suburban New York until retirement.
Things would grow predictable and, in that sense, easy.

No. I wouldn't be typing letters, but I felt that if I stayed, I
would be missing life. I had always thought of life as being
somewhere other than here. How could I suddenly switch
gears and say, "This is it, and this is where and who I want
to be"? I was still restless enough not to want this situation,
these people, to be the goal toward which I was running. But
I felt the pull of inertia weighing me down. I somehow knew

that if I didn't leave while I was still young, I would stay forever.

I had no intention of *ever* working in Manhattan, but I heard of a job opening and applied so that I could acquire more skill in fielding interview questions.

It just all happened rather quickly. I accepted the job; I resigned from my old position. Survival instinct again told me I was heading in the correct direction.

I said good-byes to co-workers who were, by now, fast friends. Because I lived alone, they were my primary local source of continuity—the people I could count on seeing day in and day out, the people who would discover me dead if I quit breathing in the middle of some night. Although this career move did not involve a change of apartments, I was in a sense leaving a quasi home, because my work, more than my place or being outside of work, defined me.

It was again time to step away from the security of the known toward an unknown land of adventure. This time the New York City skyline welcomed me.

The workdays grew longer. Commuting consumed two hours a day. Two hours to catch up on what didn't get done in the eight spent at the office. And then I read and edited manuscripts in bed at night. No one told me I must, exactly, but this was New York, and New York didn't believe that people who came there were filled with blood until and unless they spilled it.

Day after day I kept waiting to be found out. When were they going to realize that I didn't know what I was doing, that I was just a kid who was playing games that men play and whose keen ear and nose, ambition, fear of failure, and, I trusted, direction from God, told me what my next move should be?

Of those four qualities, I sensed that ambition, if left unchecked, could prove to be fatal. There was no end to the hunger of it, and, I suspected, no end to the amount of energy any company would allow its employees to expend on behalf of the corporation in pursuit of it.

Was the company replacing the central role of security and identity giver that my family had once held, that a spouse, under different circumstances, might have held?

Were a series of mentors, who were my personal and daily ties to the larger corporation, really substitute fathers or mothers or lovers who were buffers between me and the real, hard-core world?

Maybe so, and maybe individuals feel a personal responsibility to those who work for them, but, on the whole, corporations do not. Like some giant pump, whose purpose is one year of maximum maple syrup production, it pulls so much sap from sugar trees that it kills them in the process.

Whether the pressure to perform was imposed by myself or by others was immaterial. I saw glimpses of the fact that there had to be an end to this proving of myself, to this jumping higher and higher trying to reach a plateau where I finally and ultimately would know who I was in relation to myself alone and where I finally and ultimately would like the person whom I described when referring to myself.

I sat in my high-rise office, overlooking the East River, the Fifty-ninth Street Bridge, and Queens. It was winter; the sun had set early and the reflection of the moon splashed across the river.

So this was it. The life and the success I had been waiting and working for. I was my career. Though I looked and often felt frail, I had proven myself as a fighter and a survivor.

I no longer felt like fighting if more of this same was what I was fighting for. Each morning I made a practice of praying while I walked from the curb into the office building lobby and to the appropriate bank of elevators. Each day's prayer was the same: "Lord, please, just help get me through this day. Help me to concentrate on doing what must be done today, and not worry about all that I'm not getting done." I attempted to list off those things that couldn't wait. Looking at my calendar one day at a time seemed manageable. Every day involved doing what couldn't wait until tomorrow, plus chipping away at the huge block of work that could, but probably shouldn't, wait another day. The chipping away was endless.

I looked out the window and tried to imagine myself without my job. My mind went blank, and the coming of the blackness pushed my desire to live through the closed window. It was the first and only time I had no hope for tomorrow.

This office, this corporation, would not suffice as a home. I would still have to look elsewhere.

Lynn wondered what would become of her. Would she gain the whole world and lose her soul? To survive she felt as if she had to kill the woman inside of her. She often thought of the main character of C. S. Lewis' novel, *Till We Have Faces*—the princess Orual, who became queen when her father left this world. The novel portrayed her as having two distinct personalities: Orual, the princess, was ruled by love and instinct. She was vulnerable and soft and womblike. On the other hand, the newly crowned queen knew that Orual would never make it as a ruling monarch. To be successful the queen must suffocate and overpower the child and woman, Orual, who lived inside her. The queen must fight and win duels with foreign princes. In turn, she would win the worldwide respect due her title. The queen was benevolent, but not approachable, in control of every corner of her kingdom, except for the shriveling but eternal Orual, who lived, and would never die, in a sliver of her own mind. "I was mostly the Queen now," she says, "but Orual would whisper a cold word in the Queen's ear at times."

> *You are never so alone as when you turn against*
> *yourself in criticism and disgust.*
>
> W. Hugh Missildine
> *YOUR INNER CHILD OF*
> *THE PAST*

Andrea didn't know what to do with her feminine nature. There was no place for it here in the world she was in. There was no place to get rid of her emotions. Her feminine qualities worked to the disadvantage of her career advancement. If she was to stay on top of things, she couldn't be first of all concerned with nurturing or caring for other people; she couldn't wait to receive things unto herself. If she wanted something she had to stretch out her arm or even step forward with her whole body to declare that she did want it and then she had to grab it tightly before someone else took it from her.

Salesmanship was the game. She had to sell her abilities to the talent scouts. After years of waiting for the phone to ring, she had to force herself to pick it up and dial numbers that connected her to offices of people other than old friends. She had to ask for appointments, and wait through the seconds until some assistant said yes, he or she will see you, or no, he or she is and always intends to be too busy.

She could not let herself flinch at any setback—personal or professional. She had a friend who had recently lost a job; one of the many things held against this woman was that she had broken down and started to cry during a meeting in which she was being ridiculed.

One afternoon when Andrea heard that one of her co-workers had been fired, she started to cry. Because she was fond of her, yes, but also because she knew it could just as easily have been herself. Andrea's boss, an older woman, saw Andrea's red, overflowing eyes and banished her to the women's room until she could get herself together.

"I'll not put up with that kind of foolishness here in this office," the mentor had told her. "People lose their jobs. They find new jobs. Business goes on. If you're going to cry, it has to be behind closed doors."

Andrea went into the restroom, cried her eyes out, and went back the the job, wondering what kind of world she had walked into.

She was beginning to wonder whether whatever drove her had her best interests at heart, or whether, indeed, it had any heart at all.

Gail Godwin
A MOTHER AND TWO
DAUGHTERS

Christian women have to decide if we can handle our threatening of Christian men, who often don't want a too professional woman by their side. Then we have to

learn to pretend to be male or just like a man in the
secular field. So, part of the time we're restraining our
initiative (or feeling guilty and/or confused when we
don't) and the rest of the time overplaying our hand in
order to get our bosses to notice us.

Holly, single, age thirty

While gurgling a jar of applesauce
into a Corning Ware bowl,
Andrea asks if her mother
would feel slighted
never having a grandchild.

Mrs. Baker, her eyes fixed
on the ham she is cutting,
says what she feels doesn't matter
and asks if Andrea
would be happy
never having a child.

She had made it. Betty was thirty-two, and managed a department of professionals. She owned her own home. An independent woman. She claimed she hadn't thought of marriage since she was twenty-three, when a fiancé had walked out her door never to call or return.

She described herself as happy, yet one day she plopped herself into a co-worker's guest chair and started crying because she wanted a child. Where was this yearning coming from? She had never consciously wanted children. She never admitted wanting anything but what she now had. And now that she had it, it wasn't enough. She had a house and now it seemed right that it should be filled with love.

She suspected she had been fighting this off for years, burying her feminine nature while pursuing responsibility.

It occasionally surfaced and made her do things that, after the fact, mortified her. In bed at night she sometimes looked back over a day's work. She saw how unprofessional she had acted in a specific situation. She had been downright flirtatious—something she hated seeing in other women—in a place where only straightforward business dealings were appropriate. At the time she had reverted to teenage antics, even giggling, that disgusted her rational mind. Nevertheless, its seemed out of her control as well as indefinable.

It was not something she cared to live completely without. If she didn't "light up" occasionally, her life became too predictable. The existence of this other side of her didn't upset her as much as did its intensity. The power of it over herself and the instant power it gave her over men frightened her. It was something she must try, at all costs, to deny and lock up but never kill, in the same manner that Mr. Rochester, in *Jane Eyre*, had confined his insane wife to the attic. If it ever were to escape, it could destroy everything.

Some indiscretion might destroy her reputation, but, seemingly as bad as that, some legitimate falling in love with a person or with life itself might pull her mind and energy away from her work. The act of falling might kill her concentration and intensity. She had seen it happen to other women; she took singing lessons and her teacher repeatedly warned her that falling in love would ruin any chance she would ever have to sing professionally. She knew artists whose work had fallen apart the day they had lost their hearts to something other than their medium of expression. If she were to let this feminine nature escape from its tower, even if that were to happen exclusively between the hours of five and midnight, or only on weekends, might it destroy the whole life she had now built around herself? Would she hold her position, or be given the next promotion due her, if she weren't working ten hours a day, six days a week? That's what it was taking for her to keep ahead.

What would the vice-president for whom she worked think or say of her if she, for once, took two consecutive weeks of vacation and left no phone number where she could be reached? Would he accuse her of growing soft or lax or disloyal? If she allowed herself to enjoy herself—or others— would she like what she felt so much that she would let this mini-empire of an office slip, like water, through her fingers? And if that happened, would she have regrets—either regret that she had wasted her twenties on something that, in the context of love and her new life, seemed so empty, futile, and useless, or regret that she had given up something as concrete as fame or fortune for something as fanciful as life or love?

Striving for some form of recognition of worth seems like a portico through which we must walk on our way to peace with ourselves. The knowledge of having achieved a goal, any goal, brings its own satisfaction, an increase in our understanding of our own capabilities, likes and dislikes, and courage to take the next step toward being who we must be. Although reaching a goal will bring these satisfactions it may not bring the contentment it had seemed to promise.

It is success which disappoints us because we had so thoroughly expected it to be the crown of life.
                                                        Emilie Griffin
                                                        TURNING

The "twenties" are the hardest years for single women. The older you get, the easier it becomes.
                                        Encouragement given by a
                                        fifty-year-old single woman

FOUR

⬚

CALLING
A TRUCE

THE MONSTER DREAM

Its breath streams hotter, closer;
mine, though more and more fierce,
grows colder, further removed,
hardly capable of sustaining
this endangered life.
Its rhinoceros head strains
at its brontosaur body, charging,
playing follow the leader
in my miniature footprints.
He has chased on my heels
before, other nights
filled with terror.
But this full moon
will see victory, not
a consumption aborted
by consciousness.

Death, I say, must not strike
from behind, but
squarely in the face,
and, before second thoughts take hold,
I turn and brace myself
against the fall.

It stops. The monster's pursuit
halts in its tracks and
the panic from my eyes
leaps into his.
Like a balloon leaking
its gases, the leather hide
shrinks to the size of a bulldog,
and then, as a truce pact,
he lifts a front paw,
asking me to shake.

Do the riskiest thing. Take the choice that demands the most creativity, challenge, trust in God. Even if you don't know where it will lead.
Advice remembered by a young woman

I have always believed that God has a great work for you to do and I still do. My faith is in you and in God. Or you can put it the other way around. I pray, "Lead, kindly Light."
Letter from a father to his daughter, upon her starting a new venture

"This may be the best that things ever will be." There, *I* had said the words that I never had wanted to hear from anyone's lips. This may be my allotment of love. This may be my home. This may be my work. This *I* with whom I am dissatisfied may be the only *I* that I ever know.

Someone else may not walk into my world and carry me off to a home he has prepared for me; he may not even let me take his arm as we walk off and into a home of our own; he may sit in a car with the windows rolled down and amusedly watch as I dance off by myself and settle into my own "very fine house." But to be capable of "dancing off" I must quit sitting and waiting for him to come and lead the way, just as I must quit burying myself behind a professional persona whom I hate.

I was nearly thirty and I saw that this acceptance must come as a part of the natural progression of reaching toward a permanent home—something more permanent than the corporate ladder. It was again time to make a choice that would move me toward rest.

I saw four options set before me: I could, I supposed, continue just as I was, living in a furnished apartment where nothing was mine to do with as I pleased, where I could decorate only as much as the landlord's mishmash of furniture, carpets, and nonexistent color scheme allowed. Like the single women who spend their entire lives living out of cardboard boxes and suitcases, I could stay in this limbo where my profession was the only part of me that was tangibly mine—and a part of both my present and my future.

I could move back to the town in which my family lived and there settle into the life-style I had previously known. I knew women who had seen this as the answer.

One such woman looked back on her decision to return to her hometown, after working in New York City for several years, by writing these reflections in her journal: "I have felt cheated sometimes by my move back here. Rough, painful adjustment. [My] family can't provide the support of friends and peers I left [in New York]. But sometimes it's been my fault in lingering with my memories rather than choosing to act to fill my needs in the present. C. S. Lewis' *A Grief Observed* comments that we tend to idealize the past. We must weigh, pray, visualize the choices, and act, accepting the consequences. . . .

"I equated New York in some ways with freedom from my past. It was an escape of sorts. . . . But I was also incomplete. Standing fragile against the winds. Barren.

"Seems in some ways like I've recently been suffocating on my roots."

And another journal entry: "Why am I here? For wanting to share my *joie de vivre* with Mom and Dad? Is it too great a sacrifice to want that kind of relationship with them if, here, I can't fulfill my career and personal goals?"

After having returned she saw that it had been necessary, but not necessarily permanent, and possibly the cause of as many problems as she had left behind. She had been looking at herself "from the distance of memory" (Hilma Wolitzer, *Ms.* magazine, January 1982). She was learning firsthand what Thomas Merton had written—that we must know the past before we can understand the present. Getting a firm grip on her past was helping her to sort out the present; was she really where she belonged or where she wanted to be? Her parents would someday die and she would no doubt live on, who could know, possibly husbandless and not necessarily with a career she enjoyed. Time would tell whether she had solved the future's major life problems by going back home.

A third home option would have involved aggressively seeking a (possibly any) compatible husband.

Gail made this choice. At thirty, she taught high school French in a Boston suburb. During her first years of teaching, she had shared apartments with other women. But, needing to have space of her own, she had lived alone since she was twenty-five. Until her thirtieth birthday her life had followed a path that she could tolerate. After college she had known she did not want to go back to her parents' home. She had earned a master's degree and landed a challenging but not demanding job. She lived moderately yet comfortably, and dealt well with the present situation.

But the loss of her "youth" brought panic into her psychological system. She had prepped herself for her twenties. She had no inner resources left to carry her, in this same lifestyle, any further than twenty-nine. She had paid her dues. Life, man, God owed her the security of knowing that the rent would be paid if she chose not to work. She wasn't sure she wanted children, but she wanted to have the opportunity to make that decision; she didn't want it made for her by default. She no longer wanted to have to fight to hold her head above water in every arena of her life. She was tired. If she could somehow put her feminine nature, her personal life, into a permanent state of rest, then this would give her the strength she needed to fight for an administrative position—for whatever she chose to do in the next twenty or thirty years.

She made up her mind: she would find a husband. She feared she had already waited too long; all the good ones would have been taken. But yes, she did find one—at a local church that was known for having a relatively young congregation. She chose to leave a more established, family-centered church to go where available men were a part of the church's singles group.

He was not the one whom Gail had dreamed of marrying. He did not have a college education, nor the looks or personality that commanded the attention of all eyes and ears at any party. He was a carpenter—well respected for his craftsmanship. He thought things through very carefully and logically, but slowly. Too slowly as far as she was concerned. She was a moviegoer; he was a book reader. She liked jazz; he liked classical music. At first she wondered if their differences would drive her to distraction. On the other hand, he was kind, a good man. She would trade in her dream man for this gentle one and live contentedly in a home they made together.

At times Gail was all too aware of the high standards or hopes she had dropped behind her skirt, but, like Etta in *Butch Cassidy and the Sundance Kid*, she knew she could no longer afford to be as particular as women ten years younger than she.

She married. Happily. With no regrets. And her husband became her home.

Betty, the woman described in the preceding chapter as "having made it" in the corporate world, also married before her thirty-fifth birthday, although it seemed more an accident than a calculated search-and-find mission.

Her fear of losing herself intensified as she was in the process of falling in love. Her old career priorities, which were in a sense her foundation, were crumbling. But with her permission. Her choice to marry did modify her management career, but it did not destroy it.

By not having purposely decided for or against marriage, she daily put one foot in front of the other. She daily put off the decision to tell her love to leave until she woke up one morning knowing that he was as much a part of her as was her work. She was willing to gamble and in the end gave up neither.

Betty, although she did marry, seemed to have discovered a fourth home option. She did not choose to stagnate, return to her hometown, seek out a husband. She started establishing a home for herself, a physical and emotional place where she felt at rest. This place was separate from her employment—a place that would be hers even if she retired, if her work were taken from her, or if she were transferred. Buying her own house and furniture had pointed her in that direction, but for her it was a long distance from her contentment.

A part of this last choice must include acknowledging the fact that men may always be peripheral to one's self. The soul mate who would complete that part of you which is missing may or may not walk in. If "I" someday becomes "we," fine, but if it doesn't, "I" should not feel cheated out of the safe, loving, permanent resting-place called home.

At first titled *The Day the Hope Died*
Later titled
THE EVOLUTION OF A DREAM

Facing south
on a northbound commuter train
I read Joyce Carol Oates' latest
And one God-ordained sentence
blurs my thirty-year-old
just-
out-
of-
reach
Cinderella dream into mist.

Hours later
I lie exhausted across my bed
and stare dry-eyed
at the white ceiling that once
was a screen
featuring moving pictures of a palace
with a curly-haired queen and
I see a New York office
with a curly-haired manager
sitting behind a desk
reading the *Times.*

I too changed my dreams for the future, although not deliberately or consciously. It evolved, and seemed as inevitable as the dawning of any new day. I was reading a book and something struck home. It was primarily an acceptance of my sexuality, a realization of the fact that to be happy I would have to quit fighting my female nature, my anima. Being fully female while single and unattached seemed a curse greater than I wanted to bear, and one I hardly understood. Mother's model of femininity had included the coming of the prince, Cinderella's savior. Without that I felt that my femininity was wasted and of no use. I wasn't sure any other model existed but I knew I couldn't step backward, continuing to hate the part of me that wanted security more than risk, the part of me that wanted intimate laughter and the romance of life. I should be able to explain more fully what hit me that night, but I have not reread and have no intention of rereading the Joyce Carol Oates passage that delves into a husbandless woman's psyche. I fear, on the one hand, that it will hit me again with the same furor and force as it did the first time. And although I do not wish I could have bypassed the first encounter, it was painful enough that I do not want to walk into it a second time. On the other hand, I fear that I may reread the whole book and not find even one sentence that is recognizable as the one that had deep signficance for me then or as one that has any significance now. I neither want to repeat the experience nor give myself occasion to question its validity. I want the deathday of the old "hope of things happening to me as they happened (or as I wish they had happened) to my mother" to remain as a memory of healing value.

That day, when I looked into the future and saw myself as real and whole yet still single, was the day I began to view my current surroundings as possibly permanent, yet possibly full of hope, possibly within my power to change. It was the day I started making more active choices. No. I still chose not to look for a husband who was less than the fulfillment of my dreams. I would choose to look for ways to make who I was and where I was a home, a place of comfort. I would eventually decentralize my life—away from my work. I would trust that God would direct my steps.

There is no coming to consciousness without pain.
Carl Jung
CONTRIBUTIONS TO
ANALYTICAL PSYCHOLOGY

"Sometimes I still fear that I am Band-Aiding the sores. Maybe a home of my own will never quite be enough. Maybe I will always wish that I had loved and been loved enough that spending the rest of my life with 'him' was the only reasonable alternative. Maybe I will always, here and there, snitch a daydream into a future that is somewhere other than here or with someone who says he will never leave, and who is therefore, in that sense, mine. I really don't want my life to end when I retire at age sixty-five."

Mandy started rambling, but told of recently meeting a woman who had always been single, who had worked in a secretarial position until retirement, when she quite unexpectedly started hearing from a co-worker from years back whose wife had, two years before, passed away.

"They married," Mandy said. "You should have seen the light in that woman's eyes—in both his and her eyes. I mentioned how radiant she looked, and she agreed that she had never been happier. 'I had made retirement plans,' she told me, 'but marriage came along just at the perfect time.' She was thoroughly delighted to be sharing these years with someone she loved. And she didn't seem to mind at all that marriage meant giving up her apartment and moving to a town she'd never before lived in.

"It was one of those situations where her choice seemed obvious."

Mandy returned the conversation to her own "it's beginning to look like forever" situation. "I'd much rather be where I am, moderately content, capable of dealing constructively with the present, and guilty of occasionally staring into space and conjuring up a picture of the prince of my dreams riding toward me over the horizon, than stuck in an unhappy marriage that I knew was a lifelong mistake. I'd rather hope for something I know might happen to me than for something I could in reality only hope would happen to my daughter."

But yet another chain of bondage must be broken. Rationally knowing you must face the present as if it were the future is one thing; knowing that you cannot do this without facing the past is another matter.

How thick is blood
when its smell
forever lingers in the air
and its color

nightly plasters my dreams?
Is there a bleach
that dissolves such red stains
without burning, like acid,
a hole to my marrow?

*In a world that William James has described as "a
buzzin', bloomin' confusion," it is comforting to have
some unchanging entities to cling to, to be able to go on
thinking of good old, or bad old, Mom or Dad, as the
case may be. . . .*

*In a sense we [parents] are invisible to our children,
since we exist only in their heads as images fastened
firmly in place.*

Elinor Lenz
ONCE MY CHILD . . .
NOW MY FRIEND

*To grow up it is necessary to forgive your parents.
When you do not forgive them, it means you are
clinging to them in the hope that, if you can make
them feel guilty enough, they will finally come through
with more parenting.*

Chaplain Henry T. Close
PRACTICAL PARENTING newsletter

What caused the anger that contained me day and night,
that so tightly corseted my laughter? Its bind was so deep
that fiery words had no chance of escaping. At the same
time, the feeling was so close to the surface that it was a
constant effort to keep the words from spilling forth.

If someone had asked me the object of my anger, I would
have said, "The world," not wanting to dig deep enough to
uncover the cause of my unhappiness. I might have been
able to admit, "They lied to me" or "They should have told
me how hard this was going to be," but no more than that.
No more than a cosmic complaining against everyone older
than I. It haunted me, haunted me until one particular night
in my twenty-seventh year.

There was no reason for my not being able to sleep. Work

was going well. I was staying over, spending the night in Manhattan, visiting a friend in whose home I always felt at ease. Her childhood had been similar to mine—a rarity in New York—and her company was always a familiar comfort.

I tossed and turned and stared out the window at the apartment across the street, when all of a sudden the knowledge hit. It was Father who had bound me. He had raised a half-breed, a frightened girl who wished someone would come and save her from this workaday world, and a tough businesswoman who innately knew how to succeed.

It was Father who had given a green light to both the opposing "come and save me" and the "I can do it myself" characteristics, never realizing how difficult life would prove to be for women who tried to straddle the fence. It was he who had not made the choice of roads more obvious. It was he whom I hated.

I rolled over in bed, trying to turn my back on what I had just learned or rather what I knew would be my next major life decision. I could do two things: I could go on hating him. If that were my choice, I knew the rest of my days would be preceded by sleepless, nightmare-spotted nights. And that my laughter would always choke inside my lungs. Ah, but I would still have him to blame.

My second option was to forgive him. I could let go of the hurt feelings. After all, it hadn't been intentional on his part. He hadn't set out to ruin my life; if he had, my intense resistance to absolving him of guilt might have been rational, but still my struggle consumed me. I held on to my grudge as if it were a lifesaver and I a floundering swimmer who had spent every last ounce of energy.

If I could keep hold of this notion that he was responsible for my unhappiness, I was not accountable for my condition. But if I forgave him and released his hold on me, I would have to face the future and decide for myself what or who I wanted to be.

And who *would* I be if I were no longer angry, for my anger, in a sense, defined me. Without it I might become boring. I might lose my creativity. I might lose my intensity, which I saw as some kind of wall that kept me separated from the rest of the world. I would have to deal with the hole that would be left when the anger vacated. And the size of the hole frightened me.

I got out of bed and paced, thinking that if I were fully awake the bad dream would leave. But I had not even approached the limbo of near-sleep and walking did not help.

A Bible verse hanging over from childhood Sunday school drills slipped from the air into my mind: "I have set before you life and death, blessing and curse; therefore choose life" (Deut. 30:19). The last phrase remained and repeated.

What kind of choice was this—life versus death, blessing versus cursing? No choice, really. No choice at all. And in that instant I walked through death to face life. Freedom. A parent's hold was gone. I unclenched and opened my hands, welcoming the joy that flooded in replacing the anger.

The price that has to be paid for finding truly personal life is a very high one. It is a price in terms of the acceptance of responsibility. And the awareness of responsibility inevitably leads either to despair or to confession and grace. More is needed than the good intentions of the humanist. What is required is a new outlook, a personal revolution, a miracle.

Paul Tournier
THE MEANING OF PERSONS

Margaret dreamed she had gone berserk and was on a rampage, stabbing, one after another, a roomful of strangers. The last one she remembered striking was no unknown face; it was her father. She didn't want to kill him, not even hurt him. But someone other than herself was in control of her hand. She begged her father to grab her wrist and make her drop the knife. She knew he was stronger than she and could easily stop her.

But he just looked at her with sad gray eyes and barely whispered, "I can't. My power is gone."

He couldn't defend himself against her; she was killing the father she had known as a child. That point in this dream is the only time Margaret ever remembers waking herself up by hearing her own gurgling noises, which were really screams trapped in her throat.

She was calling for some other being to come and save her from herself.

And now those divine Surgeons had tied me down and were at work. My anger protected me only for a short time; anger wearies itself out and the truth comes in.

The Queen
C. S. Lewis, TILL WE HAVE FACES

In a phone conversation, my sister surprised me by saying, "You know, all we want from you is to know that you're happy. You don't have to be a success." Long ago I had established in my mind that my family's happiness would lead to my happiness. When I was what they wanted me to be they would be happy, and then, because I no longer felt the pull of their expectations, I would be content. They and I were still one connected circle, pushing and pulling each other out of sorts.

Although I was never quite sure exactly what they wanted me to be, I knew I wasn't who they had anticipated. They had wanted me to win at something. Was it the parent inside me who was unhappy with myself for not winning at everything? Yes, little victories satisfied my ego temporarily, but for an extremely short period of time. There was always the next obstacle to overcome. And there was always the one big failure of my past to contend with—I was still single.

Maybe my two conflicting dreams—to be motherlike and fatherlike—were too large, too unreachable. I could never be either. Because I was too much like both of them, I would always be disappointed in my pursuit of either likeness.

So I would learn to be the best of both of them; the worst of neither. Instead of alternately dreaming of conquering the male or the female kingdom (and always failing), I would dream of meeting small goals in the manner that would make me best enjoy and like myself. Instead of the cosmic question of what am I going to do with my life, I would ask: What am I going to do with today? Who am I going to be today?

I sensed that if I took care of today in a manner pleasing to my conscience, tomorrow would take care of itself.

This way of thinking hardly seemed compatible with the ambitious, goal-setting, career-minded half of me, but it seemed the only way to keep peace between the two opposing players. If I would be able to go to sleep each night comfortable with what I had done that day, I would: (1) live without a sense of regret, (2) live the day to the fullest, (3) be capable of living tomorrow without worrying about yesterday.

Something about Jesus' words, "Sufficient unto the day is the evil thereof" (Matt. 6:34), seemed to fit all situations, whether good or evil—sufficient unto today is today.

This new one-day-at-a-time mind-set pulled me out from under a heavy load of worry. Very recently a man twenty-five years older than I shared with me his mode of decision-making, which seemed to complement my attempt at keeping decisions small and daily. He never made a decision before its time; he believed in calling for an "hour of decision," rather than stretching it out over days, weeks, or even months. The situation he used as an example was job hunting. He pursued, he said, all leads, went on all interviews, for he never knew. What looked at first to be the least promising position had several times proven to be just the right slot. He never made up his mind until the time came for a decision deadline—the day he had to tell someone yes or no. Mentally turning down jobs that were never offered was a waste of emotional energy and was needless worry. Repeatedly asking, "What am I going to do? What am I going to do?" was like treading water—burning calories, but bringing a destination no closer. The answer to the question, "What am I going to do?" seemed obvious—Do the next thing.

I remembered being intrigued by one woman's comment about herself. She said one of her primary goals in life was to treat everyone she met the same, to meet every person with the same persona. That meant meeting men on the same ground as she met women, and conversing with those in power over her in the same manner, with the same respect, as those who worked for her. Treating the poor as she treated the rich, and treating the humble as she treated the proud. This did not mean she repeated the same conversation with every person. She still talked about the weather with strangers, about books with anyone who was interested, about recipes with men and women who loved to cook, but in each situation she saw herself as being constant—not a chameleon who could not even recognize the person then speaking as a part of herself. In the few hours I spent with the woman I sensed that she was at peace with herself—her past, her present, and her future—and was not terribly concerned about whether or not she was living up to someone else's expectations, or even her own ambitions. She simply was.

If my sister was correct in saying that my family really didn't care (within reason, of course—my parents were concerned that their children "walk in the truth," 3 John 4), then the decision of who or what I was was between God and myself. I was free of the tie that binds.

As soon as she had said those words, I thought myself rather thick for not having deduced that long ago. My parents were good people who wanted the best for me—the eternal best for me. In their own experience they had made decisions that they knew they had to make, whether or not their parents saw things the same way as they did. If they thought about it in those terms, they would have been pleased with me for nothing less than my obedience to God as he spoke directly to me.

They had followed the voice of God to them; they should understand and respect me if I was to follow the way I saw as right.

Now, to find the road I was meant to be on . . .

Peace I leave with you; my peace I give to you; not as the world gives do I give to you. Let not your hearts be troubled, neither let them be afraid.

JOHN 14:27

PART
TWO

HOMEWARD
BOUND

FIVE

DISCOVERING HOME BASE

ON WEDNESDAY'S FAITH ON TUESDAY
OR
SUFFICIENT UNTO THE DAY IS THE FAITH THEREOF

Like manna from heaven
what you need for tomorrow
will be yours for the taking at dawn,
but will rot and grow wormy
if hoarded on Wednesday for Thursday.

*Which choice must they resolutely reject? Or what
courageous about-face is demanded of them in order
that they may yet fulfill unrealized hopes? Should they
risk everything they have in order to try to achieve
certain very much desired goals? Or, again, is it
foolishness to gamble life's present achievement against
the possibility of a particular success, which just the
same may not have any definite value? One may long
hesitate between the alternatives.*
> Paul Tournier
> *THE SEASONS OF LIFE*

*There came a day when I no longer felt I was only
losing things. I knew I was beginning to add things
onto a barebones foundation that was mine. It, and
what I was adding to it, were things I would never
lose.*
> *Journal entry of a young
> woman approaching thirty*

For I know the plans I have for you, says the LORD,
*plans for welfare and not for evil, to give you a future
and a hope.*
> JEREMIAH 29:11
> *Cindy's favorite verse, the
> year she "gambled" and moved*

What did I want? Who did I want to be? How did I permanently want to justify my existence? The questions first had to be answered by establishing what I did not want and who I did not want to be.

I did not want to be where I was. I did not want to become a "New Yorker." I sensed a suction at the core of the city. It was stronger than I. If I didn't leave soon, it would be nearly impossible ever to leave. Something about the pace was addicting.

If I left and later chose to return, fine. At least I would then have the assurance that I was stronger than the pull. The memory of yesterday's victory would give me strength to return and live above the part of the city I had once felt as a potential bondage. If independence and freedom of choice were the star assets of being single, then I would hold on to them—and not let myself be bound by the need to strive and succeed.

In short, and to turn the negative statement into a positive one, I wanted to rest in the comfort of knowing who I was no matter where I was; I wanted the assurance of knowing that a city which I had instinctively hated, which I had forced myself to learn to enjoy, was not an integral part of my permanent self-definition and identity.

I wanted to know that I was I apart from the aura surrounding the phrase "I'm a New Yorker" when it is heard by anyone who isn't. I was choosing a less frantic style of life and I trusted that it would lead to eventual happiness.

I did not know if this gamble would work. Was boredom the only alternative to a life-style filled with tension? And if so, with which would life be harder? I asked the questions but knew that only hindsight would provide answers. Even with no magic foreknowledge, I knew I would not be happy unless I tried to go where I felt I was being nudged.

Paul Tournier's statement was sinking in: "The really important thing in life is not the avoidance of mistakes, but the obedience of faith. By obedience, the man is led step by step to correct his errors, whereas nothing will ever happen to him if he doesn't get going" (Escape from Loneliness).

I moved from New York and took a step away from who I

didn't want to be, away from the part of me with whom I felt most uncomfortable, away from what seemed artificial, in pursuit of what seemed more of a natural habitat.

I accepted a job in Virginia, which looked as if it were just what I'd most like to be doing. I believed in the benefits of the company's product. I would be under less pressure from outside myself and I would determine to reduce my self-imposed pressure. It would call forth more of my creative energies. The future possibilities seemed as endless as my imagination.

I found an apartment that seemed more like home than any I'd ever had. Large southerly windows, a yard of my own, a carpet upon which I could sit cross-legged, quiet neighbors. I moved closer to what felt like a place of inner rest.

The risk involved in finding out what you want may prove to be costly. Polly, working at a New York-based publishing firm, at age twenty-six decided that she wanted to go to Europe, to L'Abri, Switzerland, to uncover the mysteries of life. She stayed there six months and then decided that she really wanted to be back in New York, back in the industry she now realized she loved and missed.

She hadn't foreseen the difficulties such a decision would cause. She succeeded in reentering the field, but at half the salary she had previously made, and it would be more than four years before she would make up the difference.

She was thirty before she was able to afford (with subsidy from her parents) her own apartment, and then it was one in which a footed bathtub was in the kitchen. She could furnish the closetless apartment with only secondhand furniture.

She had tangibly paid for her choice of leaving as a means of finding out where she belonged, but she only occasionally regretted what she had done, and those regrets were materially based—she had forced herself into a corner where she physically had to live on next to nothing—not emotional regrets.

For some women the "What do I want?" question has not involved moving from one city to another, but locally rearranging career decisions—heading them toward where they want to be in ten years—assuming no one is to come and whisk them away from themselves.

At twenty-nine, Ann quit her job at a small liberal arts college to start freelancing. The college simply wasn't paying her enough for her creative input as director of publications or for the inconvenience of working for someone other than herself. She figured it out: she could make ends meet if she were to go on her own. She already occasionally moonlighted; these clients would introduce her to others. She would make her own way, or at the least she would find rest in knowing she had done all she could to try. If it didn't work, she would go back to a more traditional form of work, but she would worry about that if and when she was spending more than she was making. For now, Ann would do what she knew she must.

The courage to quit a secure job did not fall, like an acorn, from the sky. Before she resigned she had proven her capabilities and fortitude to herself. She had reached a goal she had always seen as eternally beyond her reach: forty pounds of her had disappeared. Such a feat did not come, or, as it were, leave, without great struggle. But success breeds hope for future success, and one victory gave her the courage to face the next obstacle in her path: unsatisfactory employment.

Finding contentment in your own career niche is not always synonymous with the fulfillment of your every dream. Pam never gave up her desire to make family life her primary focus. She knew that was where she ultimately wanted to be, but the right man was not to be found—and she did want the right man. She was nearing thirty and, in lieu of a family, needed a place where she could feel useful and indispensable.

She had never been one to play political games. Being "herself" in all situations had always been a unifying goal of her life. Not until after one crucial job interview, when she was relating to her father what she had been asked and how she had answered, did she even suspect that she had given a response that might have been to her disadvantage.

"If you could have any job in the world, what would you most like to be doing?" came the interviewer's question.

She did not think long before saying, "I'd like to be raising a family."

Upon hearing her relate the incident, her father gasped and said, "You didn't really say that, did you?"

"Of course I said it," she replied a bit defensively. The thought of saying anything else had never even crossed her mind.

"And they gave you the job anyway?"

Yes they had; she joined the company as their only female manager. She has been fortunate; her refusal to play games has never been used to her disadvantage.

A woman in this frame of mind must have built up enough inner sense of self to feel (although never actually say), "I am who I am—take it or leave it." In saying what she felt she must, Pam had remained true to herself; the management position seemed a reward for her loyalty to her conscience, and her receiving it seemed out of her hands—someone else's doing.

I know that I feel health in myself when my words do not betray my heart.

Elizabeth O'Connor
LETTERS TO
SCATTERED PILGRIMS

Doing right, which you know you must, may mean change; it may mean walking straight into a management position, but it may mean typing letters for the next ten years and doing so with contentment.

Leah was trained as an interior decorator and worked in that field for several years before becoming disillusioned; her job lacked meaning. She was not where she wanted to be. She went into the homes of her clients, redecorated their walls and floors and in that way made their lives more cosmetically comfortable. But she sensed that many of them were miserably unhappy people, and she knew she was contributing little to the needs of their spirits.

She was dissatisfied with the amount of person-to-person contact she had during these vital hours of the day; she felt wasted. The restlessness stemmed from some root broader and deeper than her singleness. She wanted to feel useful in the cosmic campaign of good against evil. She sensed that being single and female meant that she might have to go looking for a battleground. She was not, by her mere existence and presence, nurturing children she had birthed nor silently feeding strength into a man's character—roles she might have been playing if she had married.

The solution to her uselessness seemed to be in changing fields of work and entering a service-oriented arena. But the only jobs available in a religious organization such as she had in mind were secretarial. She *could* type, but she hadn't admitted it to any employer in years. It was beneath her, and if she spent hours at a typewriter, she would be burying her God-given talents of creativity and administration.

But the inner voice of her conscience told her that her reasoning was pure rationalization and, for her, very wrong. Not being willing to type for a living was nothing short of pride.

She felt she was being asked to choose: was she willing to serve others in a "lowly" position or would she continue to serve her self and her ego? She was being asked to turn around, walk toward and then past her pride, and gamble that on the other side rested the contentment that comes from knowing you are where you should be; she was being asked to live without the security of her reputation.

She chose what she felt she must—to accept a secretarial position at a religious, people-oriented ministry and there serve. She sensed she would not have been able to make this choice until she had known she was capable of succeeding in her original field. One cannot give up something (in this case respect and success) until one has possessed it.

"Choosing to give up power when we have none is a meaningless endeavor," wrote Rachel Richardson Smith *(The Christian Century,* December 16, 1981). "Powerlessness is redemptive only when we give up something precious."

In making her choice, Leah knew she was gaining self-respect, and, in that sense, personal and spiritual success.

She has worked in various assistant types of jobs for some five years, and rarely struggles with the old feelings of worthlessness. "I know," she says. "It makes no sense. But for me, less was more, because now I'm spending my job-oriented hours working on something in which I strongly believe. Before, my employment was a means to an end—paying the rent and justifying my existence through creativity. Now it's part of my whole-life ministry."

At age thirty, Holly strongly felt that she was moving in the wrong professional direction. She noted that at her level of management she could "no longer simply take opportunities as they presented themselves; the way to advance (something I always thought I wanted) was to take definite steps, watch what others were doing, 'groom' myself or make sure others 'groomed' me. In other words, I had to consciously and deliberately choose a road and walk down it. I was employed in a manager's paradise. There were several 'career paths' to take, but I had to choose one or stagnate. And the job had to be all-consuming if I wanted to shine. Put that way, I became very uncomfortable. Maybe, I thought, I've been flirting with a career all of this time instead of pursuing it.

"I had grown up wanting to work, and my generation seemed to take that as meaning 'work as men do' or 'sacrifice everything to the corporation.' I've discovered that I really don't want to be a successful business executive. It all has to do with 'What is worth enduring for the long-term?' I've decided that my identity doesn't have to be as bound up in my work as I once thought. I'm trying to change that. I do think that many people can bring together their faith and work, their personal and professional lives successfully, but it was difficult for me not to feel that I had to subordinate *everything* to my profession in order to meet somebody else's (the company's) standard and get ahead.

"I had to ask myself: What goal do I have that is worth the frustration inherent in a career? Is a career as understood by society what I am seeking, or is it rather a less specific fulfillment that involves developing my talents that are possibly marketable in conjunction with my interests that possibly aren't?"

Holly "consciously and deliberately" chose a path and did not stagnate. She left the line of upward mobility and chose to look within herself for her fulfillment. She is now temporarily running a word processor, looking and working toward the day when she can define herself in terms of her avocation—writing.

Holly is not alone in struggling to find a permanent identity for herself that balances her talents with her interests; the two are not necessarily easily reconcilable. It may take years of work experience before one musters up enough self-knowledge, self-confidence, security (be it financial or personal) to make decisions regarding "what is worth enduring for the long-term."

> *A fulfilling vocation is the consequence of the acceptance of our abilities and gifts.*
>
> Patricia Ward and
> Martha Stout
> *CHRISTIAN WOMEN*
> *AT WORK*

Holly made adjustments in her career goals; others find a purpose for their existence, and a real sense of belonging, in their life "after hours."

Some have opened their homes to or grown active in a weekly Bible study or small "sharing group" that not only increases their knowledge of the Word but provides them with a small local family of friends who during the week are as near as the telephone. Members of these small groups may share intimate problems of their lives or they may simply provide a base of physical or emergency support. When moving day comes, they may be each other's packers and movers; when someone's car breaks down, they may come to the rescue; when it seems time to have someone over for dinner, this core of people are the easiest to invite.

Involvement in the lives of a few such people may bring the fulfillment, self-respect, and sense of identify that solidifies life as a whole.

Other women thrive on a ministry that is not peer-oriented. They view themselves as helpers or leaders rather than members.

As part of a community action group, Carolyn visits the prison once called Sing Sing. She meets with their chapter of the NAACP and helps the inmates formulate article ideas for a newsletter. The positive feedback and sense of fulfillment she receives from this work is vitally necessary to her feeling purposeful.

Jeri intentionally spent a year without employment. She had saved money until she had enough to pay a year's bills, then she quit her job to devote herself full time to deep introspection. During these months she learned to pull her self-identity up from the depths of her soul. But reading and contemplation alone did not fill in all the needy crevices of her mind. She needed to be giving to God and contributing to humanity something besides emotional energy.

Her ministry started with the superintendent in her apartment building. Although he had come to the States from Eastern Europe years before, he had never conquered more than the basic essentials of speaking English. She started teaching him the whys and wherefores of basic grammar and soon was directing the mouths of a classful of immigrants. She also offered to teach catechism to the children of her church parish and gave hours to visiting some of the elderly widows in the congregation.

Dawn found an outlet for service in leading her church's youth group. Lee seems to draw her life from the music-related activities of her church, although her job as a secretary in an insurance agent's office pays her bills.

Many of these "ministries" do not open doors to long-lasting and deep friendships, but are specifically outlets for service, for helping others who are in some way dealing with and overcoming disadvantages or particular needs. In giving of their experience, knowledge, and stability to enable other people to meet particular goals, such women as Carolyn, Jeri, and Dawn meet needs of their own—the fulfillment of which gives them their own niche.

I thought I had found the solution to my own restlessness—found my niche—in a sunny Washington, D.C., suburb, in a relatively easygoing office that overlooked the city skyline, but from afar. Miles of greenery separated me from the marble bureaucracy.

Until Black Monday, the day someone with more power than I declared the entire department I managed dispensable. I was being put out of work. At nine in the morning of the first of June, I was given thirty days' notice.

I was asked to keep the news to myself until 4:00 P.M., at which time I was to call a meeting for some reasonable purpose. Seven hours ticked by, second by slow second. I carried on business as I had the days and weeks before, stealing only a few minutes to make private phone calls—to my family and to a few key professional contacts.

No personal decisions were made on that first day; those business-as-usual hours exuded denial of reality. It was the next forty days that hit my home base with the force of hurricane winds.

One of my sister's first questions about my future plans was an easily phrased, "Well, where're you going off to now?"

I hardly believed I had correctly heard the tone in her voice. Did she think I just upped and moved on to a new job or city as if it were an adventure and lark? Although I had never had one regret about the moves I had made, they had been far from painless. I had spent more tearful evenings than I cared to count mourning the familiarity of New York and its environs.

Now seemed the perfect time for me to return to New York. But I wasn't ready to return and I knew that my desire to be at the center of the magnet had been simply a hard case of nostalgia. But there was no rational reason for me to stay in Virginia. My profession of publishing clustered around two or three cities, and Washington was far from being one of them. To find work in Washington, it seemed I would have to "start over." And if I were going to start over, I might as well return to the city of my childhood—the city I had chosen as my hideaway retreat years before. Father owned an apartment house there. One of my sisters lived close by, and my parents would be only two hours away. My family saw it as the only logical solution to my impending unemployment: come "home" where we can take care of you.

I cannot say I was not tempted to rent a U-Haul truck, fill it, and drive north. It was the easiest route to follow. I was not at all eager to learn "governmentese," nor was I ready to move again to an unfamiliar city.

The professional home I had made for myself had been taken from me. My plans had crumbled. Was I now to put aside my years of hard-earned independence and crawl back home, a tired, "prodigal" daughter? Had this all been some kind of game I was playing?

Of course, I needed to know that I had somewhere to go if money ran short. But in the end that assurance was all the cushion I needed to spur me on to moving one step closer to my own place—writing a book, working for myself, being independent even of office hours.

The responsibilities increased rather than decreased; no one paid me for vacation time or sick leave. Only I knew whether or not I slept through my alarm on any given morning. But loyalty to the path on which I had started to walk beckoned me to stay in Virginia and continue to build a home base that was stronger than any structured vocation.

Your place requires God and requires faith.

H. Lawrence Scott

SIX

A FAMILY
OF FRIENDS

A FAMILY OF FRIENDS

One-time strangers
linger over lunch—
once, twice,
laugh at jokes made
private by repetition,
remember, on strong days,
those who are weak,
forget, forever,
hours left unsung.

*If the relationship includes love, commitment and
continuity, well, that's the stuff of which kinship is
made. These are the people you celebrate with, confide
in, mourn with, and call at 3 A.M.*
            "Trends: When Friends Become Family"
    THE WASHINGTON POST, *December 22, 1981*

*Part of your [a child's] task is to supplement what
your parents have given you and find other sources of
parenting. You need more mothering than your mother
could give you, more fathering than your father had to
offer, more brothering and sistering than you got from
your siblings.*

            Chaplain Henry T. Close
        PRACTICAL PARENTING newsletter

A family of supporting
friends, who supplement the family of one's childhood, give
meaning and put "flesh" on this life of one's own. The real
parents, sisters, and brothers, who saw you day in and day
out for years on end, will never, must never, be replaced. But

they are no doubt far away and, by the nature of families, few in number. But there is no end to the number of friends one can make and to the amount of physical help and emotional comfort and insight they can provide. They can alternately parent you and sibling you. If they are much older, they may "professionally parent" you through years of transition.

Whatever their function, these friends are a necessary part of building a home around yourself. There are no formulas for finding them—not even any tips for where to look for them. Often they are people you are forced to be with for extended periods of time; you might work with them, attend a class with them, meet them on a vacation. They may be remnants from your college circle of friends. To be sure, they are not recognized as friends on first sight, but with the passing of time, they are endowed with that title, maybe after a lengthy argument or a wrenching conversation. Maybe they are the only ones who stick by when either success or failure pulls you away from the routine of life. In times of discovery, in times of stress, and during all those hours which are neither, their reactions to you help you define yourself; their reactions to you determine how you act in their presence. Your reaction to each of them determines whether or not your relationship is a friendship at all.

The job I had left New York for was gone, pulled out from under me. And I fell into the "arms" of my family of friends. I had been assured by higher-ups that this change in administrative policy was no reflection on my performance, but nevertheless the blow sent me reeling. I did blame myself for my condition in that I wondered what I could have done differently that would have prevented this. The night of the day I was told of my imminent demise I dreamed that someone had cut off my arms and legs. I remembered so many of the details of the dream, but for the life of me I couldn't remember whether I or someone else was responsible for the mutilation.

The automatic pilot that had kept me functioning during that workday dissolved the minute I opened the front door of my empty apartment. I knew I shouldn't see this through alone. I didn't particularly feel the need to cry but I desperately needed to talk.

Ah, the telephone. As I feverishly dialed numbers I again thanked God for Alexander Graham Bell, whose invention instantly brought seemingly dead friends back to life. I don't remember all the persons I called, but two calls I will never forget. The first call made the second one necessary, as it accentuated rather than soothed my aloneness.

I wondered if I had interrupted her during an engrossing television movie, as her mind and voice were so distant. In answer to my intitial, "I was laid off today," I heard a hollow "Oh, I'm sorry."

I stopped. That kind of "Oh, I'm sorry" was what I would have expected, even wanted, from total strangers, but from a trusted, old-time friend I expected to hear an anguished, "Ohhhhh no! What happened? How could they?" And when I didn't, my pain gushed forth. Suddenly I didn't want to tell her anything. She wasn't sorry, or at least not sorry enough to help me carry my load.

It was a short conversation since I didn't want her violating my tears.

I cried alone and then made another call, hoping, hoping that Evy would come through. Come through she did. As I emptied my failure and fear in her lap, she started to sniffle. Her tears on my behalf filled my emptiness with the comfort of her presence.

Although that night's dream was violent, I woke from that sleep knowing I could live without arms and legs. Life would be difficult but such dismembering would not cause death. With "family"—whether related by birth or not—who cared enough to cry with me in bad times, I would not soon starve.

I thought back over my relationship with friends such as Evy. What had brought us close? What had melted a relationship between co-workers that started, at best, as an uneasy truce into one that prompted long-distance phone calls such as this, and as hers to me, some months before in the middle of the night, to tell me that she had just said, yes, she would marry him?

Trust, it seemed, had grown from mutual vulnerability.

The "What, you too?" discoveries that C. S. Lewis described in *The Four Loves* were multiple and frequent. The confrontations that at first threatened both of us brought us to a better understanding of why she or, in turn, I seemed so crazy. We emotionally stretched each other, told each other that we weren't as young or stupid or ignorant as we feared we were. We kept reminding each other that getting through the day was possible, even probable, and that today's strength would make tomorrow's struggles easier. (This always seems so obvious when giving advice to anyone other than yourself.)

But that wasn't all, for her laugh was infectious. On the streets of Manhattan at lunchtime we would giggle like girls on their way home from school. And then we would laugh at our laughter and tell each other to grow up because we had to go back to the office.

I think of all the friends of the heart I have known, the people who for a while, if not for always, have known how I think and what I'm thinking, some to a greater depth than others. None of them became trusted friends after one warm or intense conversation. It was when one little piece of self was shared and not violated that I, if and when the opportunity arose (and part of the effort of gathering a family of friends is enabling those opportunities to arise), shared another little piece, and then another, and another—all the while listening to their secrets. In between laughing and crying with them I inwardly smiled, assured, that I was not nearly as alone as I once thought.

For some women the idea of trusting other women enough to reap the harvest of their support is anathema. They have viewed their own kind as the competition—for men and job advancement. Throughout their high school, college, and first working years, they could never be too sure: would the center of their heart tomorrow be stolen by yesterday's friend? And most women can in some sense identify with such a thief; most women know all too well the fountain of evil dormant, if not bubbling, in other women. They suspect that it can for years lie still as a stagnant pool, but that if the right switch were pulled it could skyrocket into a vertical stream that would destroy all semblance of the once peaceful and horizontal surface.

On the other hand, there are a few women who are blind to such fickleness. Over an extended period of time I observed one woman's outlook on life. She trusted everyone she met and assumed that everyone, acquaintances as well as proven friends, was as loyal as she herself.

Trusting no one leads to extreme alienation; trusting everyone leads to sure betrayal.

Do I count on my friends' eternal support? Of course I do, but of course I don't.

I was surprised that the minister giving Evy's wedding homily found some truth in the much-berated line from the movie *Love Story:* "Love means never having to say you're sorry." But he spoke highly of it in terms of love's ideal motive as found in 1 Corinthians 13:7: "If you love someone . . . you will always believe in him, always expect the best of him, and always stand your ground in defending him" *(The Living Bible).*

We should assume that those closest and dearest to us will always put the interests of our friendship before their personal interests. We should assume that they always act in love.

To be made as thick as blood, water must be fortified with enormous amounts of testing, vulnerability, pain, and finally trust. I expect all my best friends to be those who would, as Jane Howard describes in *Families,* "swim rivers and go sleepless for weeks" for my sake. But at the same time, I keenly remember the story of Peter's denial of Jesus—just a few hours after saying he would stay loyal through death. I remember hearing the stories of lepers once loved who became outcasts because of their sudden uncleanness. I think of nursing homes and prisons that are filled with people too much like myself, people who once knew that their friends would never leave.

"You expect too much from your friends," an observer once told me. "You've got to learn that friends come and friends go."

And so I have; but I never expect them to. I have watched and cried as friends have emotionally left. I'm not sure that it ever becomes easier, if one ever hardens or should harden to the blow of deaf ears, silent lips, and mute laughter, of "please call" messages left unheeded. Friends leave easily only when not too much of yourself goes with them.

Why do friends leave? Sometimes marriage or the prospect of marriage consumes them, especially when the struggles of singleness or aloneness seem the strongest thread weaving your friendship together.

This, I remember, seemed to be the pattern with college friends who married before they were twenty-five, before they had developed a firm sense of who they were as individuals.

ENGAGEMENT ANNOUNCEMENTS
FROM COLLEGE FRIENDS

They say
they've found their resting-place.

One has given away Kristofferson
and bought Schubert.

One says
she's through with the shrink.
One never makes decisions,
Peter does it for her.

I have known their restless years.
Cried
Complained
Walked
Reasoned with them,
Spent sleepless hours
Listening—again.

I miss the storm,
Don't recognize the calm.
They notice my silence,
Ask where I've gone.

Who leaves whom in such situations is not the important issue. Marriage, whether early or late, brings changes. By definition it rearranges priorities. One's mate becomes one's first human concern; old friends must step back. But I think not as much as some engaged women think.

A letter from one of my friends shares the pain of the marriage of another close friend: "I feel sort of cast off by Jane. I only had one very meager note from her since Christmas. She doesn't seem to depend on my correspondence or the fact that I'm thinking about her a lot, as I do on hers. Or, at least, she doesn't seem to realize how much I need it. I just don't feel at all necessary to her. And she gives me no reason to believe otherwise. I guess I just feel sort of hurt, even though I realize that she maybe isn't to blame—for her marriage to work she needs to find that friendly intimacy with him that we have had and that takes a real investment of time and energy. But no matter what I *know*, I can't help *feeling* abandoned. . . . This feeling has made a difference in my writing to her, too—I don't bother to tell her everything like I used to, since it really doesn't seem to be important or make any difference. I *hate* to see this happening."

Where are the plans for a picnic for three? Where on the schedule is a walk, a lunch, or a shopping trip for two—your old friend and you (and when he's out of town doesn't count)? Madonna Kolbenschlag defines the point of tension in this female/female conflict precisely: "Friendship with a woman is sustained only when it does not conflict with or threaten the important male relationship. Every woman knows what it is to be 'ditched' on an evening by a female friend, when that significant 'One' phones" *(Kiss Sleeping Beauty Good-bye)*.

To let friendship die away by negligence and silence, is certainly not wise. It is voluntarily to throw away one of the greatest comforts of this weary pilgrimage.
Samuel Johnson

I am as responsible for rejoicing with those of my friends who call me in the middle of the night to tell me they are marrying as they are responsible for weeping, a month later, with me for the children I may never have. A friendship that can walk through both of those doors without cracking from the threatening pressure brings intense joy.

Esther Harding quotes a Chinese sage: "All association on

the basis of common interests holds only up to a certain point. Where the community of interest ceases the holding together ceases also, and the closest friendship often changes into hate. Only when the bond is based on what is right, on steadfastness, will it remain so firm that it triumphs over everything" *(The Way of All Women).*

And only time tells which friendships are based on truth; which, even though broken for a while, will find a new springtime. Some are destined like a good marriage to withstand arguments, jealousies, even the blackest pain, but only when love is not possessive.

"I have done all I can do," Jo Ellen said to herself. One friend whose emotional presence she thought she needed as much as her hands, left. Always too busy. Never returned calls. No reply to her "What's wrong?" queries. Was it her fault?

It seemed not; she had tried, tried to reconcile the break. Sometimes, she realized, people leave for no reason whatever. She opened her hand, let the friendship go, but not without great anguish.

But years later the friend returned through mutual friends to be a part of Jo's casual social circle. On the first encounter of reacquaintance, Jo could think and feel nothing but "You owe me an apology."

There was no spoken apology on that first meeting, but a look in her friend's eyes pleaded forgiveness. A spoken "Thank you"—with no objective clause hung to the end of the sentence—was all Jo heard.

Jo's asking "Thank you for what?" was unnecessary. She had let her friend go when the time for leaving seemed necessary. As parents must let go of their children, as the father let go of the son who was called prodigal, as God will not force our will, there comes a time when those who do not return our phone calls must be released, but welcomed back if and when they choose to return. The whys of their leaving can be dealt with later, or maybe never, for as Albert Schweitzer said, "A man must not try to force his way into the personality of another. . . . The soul, too, has its clothing of which we must not deprive it."

They must be let go and then welcomed back, knowing

that we have not always been faithful. If they never come back (or in the meantime), our memories must hold the laughter we shared together more tightly than the tears we have shed alone. The memory of laughter can bring old friends near.

The friends, the new family, should ideally include children, men, and women of all ages.

The spontaneity of a child springs a refreshing stream of wonder into the driest of lives. Jane Howard reflected on her own experience: "To hold a snuggling, trusting child on one's lap is to feel a deep and peaceful intimacy as necessary, to me at least, as any feeling I know" *(A Different Woman).* Teacher Margaret Clarkson thanks God that he "graciously met my own deep need to nurture by plunking me down in a classroom for thirty-eight years. . . . Today I have children and grandchildren everywhere" *(So You're Single!).*

Although the presence of children can sometimes make me later more acutely aware of the absence of children of my own (when I experience no contact with children for long periods of time, I do not miss them much; it is when I see a baby that I wish one existed that were half me), their presence nurtures a necessary abandonment of all but the most basic concerns. Their attention and affection is free, although not to be sought out today and disregarded tomorrow.

The words of a child can even advise and give worthy insight. My five-year-old friend, J.C., recently overheard my conversation with her mother. Nothing was going right, I complained. I just didn't seem capable of . . .

J.C. interrupted in the middle of the sentence, as she so often does. Her tone of voice prompted gales of laughter, and her words dissolved my lamentation. "Oh, Evelyn, Evelyn, Evelyn," she bemoaned, "what *are* we going to do with you? Can't you see . . ." and she made the problem seem as petty as an argument over who gets the biggest piece of cake.

Children, fine, you say. But what's to be done with the male companion who, for one reason or another, *must* remain in that safe warm zone of "friends only"? He is a necessary part of the built-up family—the brother who shares a part of your life, your work, exercise, or hobby. Maybe he's married; maybe he knows you're not "the one"; maybe you know he's not "the one." Whatever the reason, some relationships must not be defined in permanent or "romantic" terms, yet that doesn't seem to short-circuit the sexual attraction.

Neither I nor any women I talked to have had any answers to this dilemma short of sheer willpower, the Spirit's constant reminder of the selflessness of love, and the grace of God.

> *Sexual feelings are present in many interpersonal relationships and should not be frightening. Sexlessness and coldness are not the measures of holiness. Friendship between the sexes involves sexual feelings, yet genitality does not become a primary mode of communication. . . . A mature person knows when he is communicating affection and when he is arousing genitality.*
>
> *Donald Goergen*
> *THE SEXUAL CELIBATE*

An affirming or comforting kiss or hold can salvage the worst of days. And burying one's self in someone's arms for a good cry can bring as much release as an orgasm.

In such friendships, highly valued by both parties, attempts can be made to keep the companionship nonexclusive. If he is married, do you share as openly with his wife as with him? If he is not married, do you allow for the fact that he has or should have other friends with whom he may share as much or more of himself as he does with you? While he may satisfy many of your emotional needs, do you still seek out other "family" members with whom you can share your dreams and disappointments?

If or when these seem impossible strides, such relationships may have to be defined verbally. If definitions provide no help such attachments may have to be broken, for "hope deferred makes the heart sick" (Prov. 13:12). But ultimately, only an individual can decide how much tension he or she is willing and able to live with and whether or not such a relationship is helping or hindering his or her personal growth.

What good is a roomful of chairs if no one ever sits in them? And what good is a cityful of friends if none of them ever remembers your birthday, that once-a-year dawn that has the power to bring on a depression as black as the air underneath a comforter at the strike of midnight?

It's not *only* that on this day, as on New Year's Day, monster time threatens to cat me whole. It's that this day, like Christmas, is always a promise of sweets and scarlet. Why is it that no matter how expensive the chocolates received or how red the roses delivered, they are never quite as flavorful or colorful as the desserts and gifts remembered from childhood?

It's not that my birthday memories from younger years are so vivid and distinct; they have all blurred together into one round layer cake and one red fire truck. It's that the day was all mine, not shared with anyone else, as with Christmas. All eyes watched while I opened presents. The family sang to me. I blew out candles lighted in honor of my birth.

No dose of rationality has been strong enough to kill my high hopes for the day. But as much as I crave attention I find it nearly impossible to ask for it. If friends cannot remember on their own, their greetings are worth no more than the paper upon which they are printed. My reasoning is simple: My mother is a true friend. She has never had to be reminded of my birthday, therefore all true friends should remember my birthday. But I have only one mother-who-has-never-forgotten.

One quarrelsome love intentionally ignored my twenty-second and smirked a "What are you going to do about it?" smile as he walked out the door to spend the evening with friends.

The Friday before my twenty-third set me into a crying spell so severe that a co-worker sent me home to my parents for the weekend.

Not wanting to spend the weekday evening of my twenty-fourth alone, I invited a good friend from work home for dinner. In the middle of a one-sided, self-condemning dessert conversation on how hurt she would be if her friends forgot her birthday, she stopped and stared at me, mortified. "It's today, isn't it?" she gasped. "I must have subconsciously known."

We both laughed nervously and then celebrated quietly.

Another friend, recovering from a nervous breakdown, spent my twenty-seventh birthday at my apartment. Trying not to increase her already crippling load of guilt, I never told her she had forgotten the special day; I sneaked my cards off to the bathroom and read them in private.

"No more of this suffering in silence," I told myself soon before my twenty-eighth, and I campaigned for a good day. I broke all my rules and it worked: a day of aimless country driving with my love, and a candlelight dinner.

"This," I said, "will prove to be a model for all future birthdays, and the memory of each one will float me through the rest of the year."

But one year later I had no courage to subtly or directly give reminders, and the same love forgot my day with the silence of a thousand unplugged telephones.

Thirty was the big one. I again threw aside my pride by giving myself a party, inviting twelve friends for spaghetti and salad. There are times, I decided, when monsters such as time needn't be attacked head on. If they are not directly pursuing they may be allowed to nap or graze, while I on tiptoe walk around them. Diversion is sometimes an acceptable escape for those special days like birthdays, Valentine's Day, New Year's Eve that may not be worth, or when there may not be time for, a trip to your parents' home but for which you have amassed great expectations.

Spending alone one such day in a lifetime may be necessary—to prove yourself stronger than the twenty-four hours—but I now see more than one such traumatic day as unnecessary. What are friends for if not to help each other through the worst but best days of the year?

New Year's Eve—that second day when time is to be celebrated yet mourned—has for many young women proven to be a string of yearly disasters, when friends seem far away. After Christmas one year, I started asking acquaintances what they were doing on December 31. I was astounded at the number of people who shuffled their feet or papers and said, "Oh, not much; I don't like parties, you know," it never being clear whether they did not like parties or whether they had been invited to none.

I started inviting them all over. "No party," I said. "Just munching pizza."

In the end it, too, was a disaster, because the number of people involved forced the definition of a party upon it. It became increasingly more and more clear that these people really did hate parties, and a party for people who hate parties is hard to get off the ground.

I've not tried that tactic again, but then neither have I spent another New Year's Eve home alone crocheting.

December 31 is not the evening in which to prove your independence, but one in which the need for company should be acknowledged.

Some years I have swallowed all pride, called trustworthy friends and said, "I can't stand the thought of being alone. Whatever you're doing, can I come along?" Having a good sense of which friends would be doing what and which friends would feel such a question an intrusion, I have yet to be turned down. And others have asked the same of me. It's a gamble, of course. You might end up at a hated party or church service, but at least you have not stayed home and felt sorry for yourself.

Several years I have invited one or two friends over for dinner. They went home before midnight, but we parted full of the company of each other.

Why, I ask myself, does it seem that I must always take care of myself on these occasions? Why doesn't someone else call saying he or she just happened to be wondering if I had made plans for New Year's Eve, and if not wouldn't I love to join his or her commemoration?

Because I'm bad company? Because they'd rather spend their evening privately, cuddling around their own fireplace? Because they're afraid of being turned down? I've never asked them, but probably none of the above; they have probably simply never thought of it. Those who have at least one other person seldom think of a third, and those who are alone fearfully assume they are the only ones in the country who are.

For some women, neither birthdays nor New Year's prompts the yearning for attention; it is Valentine's Day that friends would do well not to forget. Pam's mother, more than most mothers, made a production of the day. Love. Sweethearts. Be mine. Special cakes and cards. Now the void is difficult for Pam to live with.

Maybe Pam has found the secret for getting past all such milestones. She tries to make the day special for other people by sending cards or making remembrances. She attempts to busy herself in giving rather than receiving, and thus she makes the day something other than the usual for more than herself.

But what's to be done with the people who always receive and never give back? It may not be that they never give a part of themselves. (They may lay all they have on your doorstep.) It may be that they take, without permission, bits and pieces of your life and limbs. The weaker are always looking for the stronger, the emptier for the fuller, and no matter how frail you may feel there will always be those who are worse off.

Although the child in me forever may be clinging to or searching for Mother's hold, the very fact that I have left her gives me strength I may not feel but that others see.

Should I welcome such leeches? Should I run from their sight to free myself to make friends that will be mutually beneficial?

Over dinner conversation, Anne mentioned how eager she was to get an apartment of her own. She had a roommate who was older than she yet who would not take care of herself. Anne woke her up every morning. (She would rise only on the third call.) Anne did more than her share of the cleaning, and Anne had become a live-in counselor. "I've just got to get out," she said. "She's eating me up."

I wince and nod affirmation all at the same time. I wince because the weaker do need the stronger, not so much as leaning posts but as encouragers and as examples. And I nod affirmation, because I have also turned my back on would-be swallowers, would-be grown-up children looking to me as their parent knowing that I at the time had only enough resources to keep myself barely alive emotionally.

I read newspaper features about the crisis of clergy burn-out—people who earn their living by loving, by overextending their inner resources to the point of fragmentation or exhaustion—yet I read of Mother Teresa who seems to have the inner strength to take on her shoulders the problems of the whole world. I feel guilty for turning even one away, for I was once and may be again in a position of being grown up yet utterly alone and terrified. I see that Jesus welcomed all who were in need, yet the same Jesus repeatedly sought hours of solitude alone with himself and his Father, away from them all. He answered their questions and touched them with love, yet he never made their decisions for them. He told them that only they could choose what they would do with their lives. He offered what assistance he could, although they did not all become members of his close family of friends.

For close companionship he chose twelve—a large, yet small number of people—with whom he became familiar and personally attached. We can and should help and love all who cross our way, for what we give to them we've given to the Lord (Matt. 25:40), but our familylike ties will be reserved for a few special people.

We all need a few good and close friends. Sometimes, in an emergency, one will do the trick. But if we . . . do not really satisfy this need, the denial will often evidence itself in the collecting of a hundred friends, none of whom are really such. The process of collecting gets to be exhausting, and each friend becomes a distraction from the other.

William F. Lynch
IMAGES OF HOPE

SEVEN

A PLACE OF ONE'S OWN

HOME SWEET NOTHING

Chairs that dot the tile floor with wooden squares
cast long shadows on beige walls
that blush in the afternoon sun
with the shame of their nakedness.
Bubbly chenille covers a narrow wrinkle-free bed
and the closet rod hangs three pairs of slacks
each a foot from the next.
In one corner a refrigerator gurgling inner fluids
freezes milk and orange juice in paper cartons,
and the cord of one electric coil
dangles from a table near an outlet.
Shades unroll halfway down curtainless windows
that once sparkled clean.

Every evening the keyhole is turned
and homage paid to the sleep-god;
every morning, the neighbors say,
what looks like a man walks out the drive.

Home, for adults, is a place that they have created for
themselves and that reflects their tastes, interests, and
life style.

Elinor Lenz
ONCE MY CHILD . . . NOW MY FRIEND

It's no way to live. His apartment seemed to say too much about the frame of his soul. As if he had left a childhood home, the room that was his own, and never found its replacement. Paul Tournier says: "One becomes a person only if one really has a place. . . . And that place is no abstraction. It is . . . the fireside, the photographs on the mantelpiece, . . . the books on the shelves, all the little details with which they have become familiar" *(A Place for You).*

The building up of this place of one's own comes with time, as one's tolerance for living in a physical state of limbo decreases and even explodes. "Home Sweet Nothing" provides no security beyond the assurance of protection from wind, cold, and rain. It doesn't replace the childhood home in any sense other than physical safety. To leave successfully the home of childhood, one must work toward building up a home that reflects his or her own interests and the tastes that gradually are viewed as his or her own.

At thirty, Susan felt as if she was "nowhere." She owned nothing but a dog, her secondhand furniture, and a car; she worked at a job that was "permanently temporary" and not in her field of training or interest. She started making plans for another major change. She had contacts with a firm in a distant city who would provide her with freelance work if she would move closer to their facilities.

For six months she sent out feelers for a compatible living situation. She did not have enough money to pay for anything more than half an apartment's rent so she had to find a roommate, and one who at least tolerated her pet which she was not willing to give up. The search for a place to live was difficult indeed, and one her parents did not seem to understand.

One telephone conversation included questions from her father about what ever could be taking her so long to find an apartment. Why was she being so particular?

"I'm thirty years old," she exclaimed. "I need a place that I feel is mine; I don't want my furniture to end up on the street. I can't just rent a room in some widow's house and feel as if I were a guest or back in college."

Her father, she said, grew strangely silent and asked her no more probing questions. Once reminded, he knew the importance of place.

When you knock it never is at home.

William Cowper
"Conversation"

I walked into Cherry's high-rise one-bedroom apartment, not having any idea what to expect. She was thirty-four, and never married, and I wondered if she would have settled into a place of her own or whether she would still be thinking of this apartment as "OK for now, until something else comes along."

The apartment was beautifully and amply furnished with bamboo and wicker furniture, and a multitude of sitting and hanging baskets, filled and not filled with plants, alive and dried. I immediately asked the question that was burning on my tongue: How had she come to have such a "together" apartment? Had it been a gradual acquisition? Had it come all at once?

Cherry laughed and said that one day she had just decided that to live a normal life she must encumber herself with the trappings of a home, but she could gather the furniture only if she still gave herself an out: if she needed to make a drastic life change, she could always have a "yard" sale and be right back where she had started—free. The buying of it did not attach or endear her to it.

Donna, a single, corporate executive, had managed to furnish comfortably her whole apartment, except her bedroom. A corner of her mind held out. She would decorate that holy sanctuary as part of the preparations for her wedding. With the input of her fiancé, she would make the bedroom into a pleasant place of retreat.

She was thirty-six before she saw the foolishness of depriving herself of the pleasure and comfort of that room which, up until that point, had given her only the pleasure of her dreams. She bought furniture, decorated to suit her tastes, and set her mind to spending time in and enjoying the large, light-filled room.

While no one's home should be an idol, it is a wise single who invests as deeply in his home as he would if he (she) were married.

Margaret Clarkson
SO YOU'RE SINGLE!

Mary, thirty years old, shares a house with a woman who owns the furnishings. Mary only claims her own bed and some of the decorations. She instinctively knows that it's time to get an unfurnished place of her own, maybe to buy a house. Her problem is no money. Cheryl, age thirty-two, wanted to buy a house, but put it off, until the tax laws seemingly forced her hand.

Although lack of money is frequently an obstacle to buying, it never need be an obstacle to setting up a place of one's own. When I moved into an unfurnished apartment, I thought that, for once, I would let the Salvation Army come to my rescue. Besides what I found there, I took anything with any hope of being fixed, painted, or stripped, from friends, acquaintances, and the curbed trash of wealthy neighborhoods. I read the local paper. I didn't let empty floor space frighten me.

I bought a double bed, that is to say, mattress and springs. If this was life, then it would include the physical furnishings of a real, adult house. Why buy a single bed, all the while thinking of it as another temporary and minimumly required measure to get me through this waiting period?

Buying the makings of this bed was a major step, as it was the first piece of furniture I owned that was, by itself, too big to fit in my car. It was delivered to me by truck. If I were to move I would have to rent a truck or a van; I could no longer rest in knowing that my car was sufficient for all my moving needs. The thought horrified me but I put it out of my mind, and proceeded with the purchase of the year. It was time to quit thinking of myself as likely to move at a day's notice, and time to provide my relatives with a place to sleep (besides the kitchen floor) should they visit me.

I crocheted chair covers and a large rag rug; I remade curtains and drapes that had been the wrong size, but that still harbored years of life. I collected plants to cover up a few of the barren spots and, after the absolute basics had been gathered, grew more particular in looking for just the right thing for each corner.

As I now replace pieces that match nothing with more appropriate decor, I pass the discards on to others who are just starting or who are somewhere along this journey of gathering things unto themselves—making themselves a home.

> Over beef en brochette
> on the upper East side
> I tell Marylou
> my parents are retiring—
> moving to a town west of nowhere.
> "Guess it's time I moved," laugh
> "all that junk out of the closet
> of my old room,"
> and as unexpectedly as the brimstone
> fell upon Sodom
> the joke blazes into fire.
> I banish myself to a woman's cubicle
> and blow, with perforated paper,
> my nose red.
> I return
> to cold coffee,
> ashamed. "How silly.
> Crying over a few
> ten-year-old dresses
> and some holey gray sneakers."

It wasn't even the house I had lived in when I was a child. It was a house, a town, they had moved to when I was a sophomore in college. I knew the names of only the closest neighbors, and had a passing acquaintance with some members of their local church. There was no one in that town with whom I felt any kinship.

So why did the phone call informing me of Father's decision to resign his administrative job and return to parish work jar me so intensely? They were moving. I knew that I shouldn't expect my parents to pack, move, and unpack my books that lined the shelves in my bedroom, the few boxes of high school memorabilia on the floor of my closet, and the few hanging dresses that I thought would come back into style if I kept them long enough.

If I couldn't ask them to move these things for me, I had to sort them myself, make a save-or-throw decision, and then transport what was salvageable to my own apartment. As long as my parents had stayed where they were, I didn't have to decide what to do with these possessions of no earthly value, other than to answer to the affirmative Mother's once-a-year question: "Do you still want all that stuff that's up there in your room?"

What did she think? That I would throw out the contents of "my box"? (All of my brothers and sisters filled their own highly treasured cardboard box with private, important mementos that told the story of their lives from kindergarten through twelfth grade.)

At the time of my father's decision, I had furnished my own apartment, but an aversion to being "tied down" still gnawed at the back of my mind. If I saved these things, my closets would be cluttered with boxes I never opened. I would have more to move—*if* (as opposed to when) I even wanted to leave.

I went home to pack about a month before Mom and Dad moved. Although I didn't see the new, out-of-town house, Mother described it thoroughly. My room, she told me, would be upstairs. But they wouldn't heat it in the winter and it surely would be hot in the summer. Of course I would want to sleep in the more comfortable first-floor guest room.

I did not want to be more comfortable; I wanted a room of my own, a place that connected me to the old house, which connected me to the house before that and the house before that. I seethed for several days.

But fortunately part of the week-long visit home was a one-day trip to my parents' cottage, a small summer house in the center of a church-owned campground. I had spent two to four weeks of every childhood summer and every Fourth of July weekend of my life at Chambers. As soon as we rode through the gates of the camp, I knew that this was the answer to my rootlessness. Here I would make a place for myself.

A small two-room cabin on the wooded edge of the camp was for sale, but shortly it was mine. Two barren rooms. Cold water running to a kitchen sink, but no toilet; the inside of the clapboard shingles, divided by unpainted studs, served as walls. The exterior paint had dropped to the ground, encircling the foundationless structure with yellow shavings. Flaunting a new roof, it was rainproof and, being surrounded by huge old trees, it was never unbearably hot. It was perfect for its purpose—easing me through the first intense sense of loss of childhood space.

I would not be losing it, I would be reclaiming a part of it for myself. In *A Place for You*, Paul Tournier wonders if "the relationship of people with places is not more stable than that with their fellow human beings." Home—the place remembered—is more than people, it is a landscape and a smell and a series of rooms that are connected by doors and windows to outside air and neighbors who come and go. It is stationary and therefore not as fickle or changeable as people who walk into and out of it. My parents may have been moving, but I firmly held on to a part of the old, more permanent place.

A month later the truck carrying my parents' belongings pulled out of their ex-driveway. The next Thanksgiving I visited them in their new home.

"I'm sleeping upstairs, in my own room," I said in answer to my mother's query. But I slept restlessly, and over coffee the next morning I accused the movers of placing the mattresses on the wrong beds. "I couldn't sleep last night because the bed was so soft. My mattress is on Philip's bed, and his is on mine," I complained.

Confident that she had properly overseen the packing and unpacking, Mother marched up the stairs and checked. "Having turned these mattresses twice a year for thirty years," she said, "I know which is which and they're right where they've been for seven years."

"Well, that surely is not the mattress that lulled me to sleep when I was a kid."

Mother tried to hide a smirk. "I put your mattress on the guest room bed seven years ago. How come you never noticed until now?"

I laughed at myself, inwardly, if not outwardly. It was only when my sense of home was threatened that I had the sensual touch of the princess who could feel the pea under her piled-high mattresses. In the absurdity of it all, I stepped back and looked at myself and at the situation: I was the renter of an apartment, the owner of a cottage. I still had healthy parents and was more fortunate than most people, in that I had many brothers and sisters who had homes of their own which were open to me. Why did I need a room in my parents' home that was mine?

Right before my eyes the problem seemed to dissolve, and permanently enough that I have not since slept in that upstairs "girls' " room. I happily sleep in the more comfortable, yet smaller and more sterile, downstairs room that is shared, in my absence, with my parents' myriad overnight visitors, or, when the house is full, I sleep on the couch.

Although I hung on to my hideaway cottage for two years, I sold it and with little sense of loss. It no longer seemed convenient to spend vacations there; by then, I had moved into an apartment owned by a woman who made me feel as if I were living in a home that was my own. My cottage had served its purpose, and I grew ready to leave it without wrenching my heart.

I now walk through my apartment, particularly noticing the heritage of its furnishings and decoration: a plant given to me by Anne, another from Vicki's deceased mother, a table scarf woven by Mrs. Triglia, a poster that used to be Suzanne's, my grandmother's sewing machine, a crewel plaque stitched by Mother, a pottery bowl given to me by Sandra, a rock I picked up on a Cape Cod beach, the chair I bartered from my sister, the grandmother clock made by my father, the pillow bought for me in Ireland.

Every room is filled with invisible threads which on lonely, stormy nights lead me to faraway friends, family, and places. They provide instant connections with parts of me as real as my fingers or my knees, yet as impossible for me to view as my inner ear.

I am here. They are somewhere out of my sight, yet vital to my sense of equilibrium and health. Some are alive. Some dead. But where they are never seems quite as important as do these physical representations of their entwined memory.

In much the same way that one builds a house, I have built a home about me. As part of my plan I accept and collect remembrances as one might collect special stones for a rock garden.

In the midst of dusting under candles and holders kept

and rearranged since college days, I see why God gave his people who were wandering in a desert a box that symbolized his presence, why he sent to earth a part of himself in the flesh, why his Son instructed his followers physically to eat and drink his remembrance, why it is so important that we continue this until he returns.

The rooms I live in, although important, seem not as vital as the few-growing-into-many things that make the place mine. I will always covet a dwelling with a front door and a back door and with some accompanying lawn—security blankets remembered from a suburban childhood, but those things do not define me as much as these other things, which constantly remind me who I am and where I have been.

It is hard to succumb to the temptation of questioning my existence when the collection of these objects proves that I have had a past. I was there. I am here, even when no physical being knows my actions or my thoughts.

My furnishings are unique. Guests walk through the front door, look around, look at me. The usual comment is not complimenting the "fine" furniture, but a warm "Your apartment looks so much like you" that makes me grateful for it and for myself.

Aunts comment on the fact that I don't seem able to control the books and the papers. Cousins comment on the framed pictures on the wall that transport one back in time.

Yet they, my guests, all seem at ease here—sensing that I and my home are one, not contradicting each other in style or personality.

Beth recently rented her first unfurnished apartment. She carefully filled it according to her tastes. The day came when her task was complete. It looked like a home. But it still seemed empty. She walked to the neighboring apartment and knocked on the door of another single woman with whom she had made acquaintance. The neighbor was surprised by Beth's question: "So, I've bought everything I need to decorate, and everything is settled in. I'm finished. Now what do I do?"

Although it was full of things she liked, the apartment did not feel like home. Decorating it had occupied nonemployed hours for several months. Now, sitting and reading a book in her newly acquired favorite chair seemed anticlimactic.

She felt somewhat like the traveler, John, in C. S. Lewis' novel *The Pilgrim's Regress*, who could not force himself to enjoy a forest that was nearly, but not quite, like the wood on an island he had enjoyed when he was a child: "He set his teeth and wrinkled his forehead and sat still until the sweat rolled off him in an effort to enjoy the wood. But the more he tried the more he felt that there was nothing to enjoy. There was the grass and there were the trees: 'But what am I to *do* with them?' said John. Next it came into his head that he might perhaps get the old feeling."

The old feeling John was looking for was "at-homeness."

"He shut his eyes and set his teeth again and made a picture of the Island in his mind: but he could not keep his attention on the picture because he wanted all the time to watch some other part of his mind to see if the *feeling* were beginning."

When, how, does the "Now what do I do with it?" question get answered? One of the most obvious replies is, "Relax. Share it. Break up the day-to-day living in it with guests who may enjoy it with you."

Some of the best times I or guests have had in my home have been over platefuls of spaghetti or omelettes—hardy royal fare. What to serve never seems the most difficult part of entertaining. If all else fails, the local delicatessen or pizza parlor can do the fussing. It's the inviting that takes so much energy.

What if I planned a party and then no one came? What if they agreed to come, but only because saying no would be impolite? What if they said, "I'm sorry, I can't come, I have to do my laundry that evening"? Then would I have to go invite the lame and the poor, like the man whom Jesus described in the parable of the banquet? Would those who were desperate for a meal be the only ones who would come to my table to eat?

It was so easy for me to pick up the phone for any reason but the one of asking a "real" family—a husband, wife, and child—to dinner. The dialing reflex should have been more automatically programmed into my subconscious. I spun the numbers. This family's coming seemed terribly important; it was to be my one planned social event of the weekend, the once in a month when I would play hostess and, by design, share my home with others.

Some would answer the phone and respond to my invitation: yes, they could come; no, they were busy; or an answer somewhere in between that was now familiar: "We'd love to see you, but it's so much easier for you to come here than for us to come there."

How they knew what was easiest for me, I'm not sure. But such an answer did not make picking up the phone the next time less difficult.

Why bother having an apartment if nobody ever comes?

> *Young single woman*
> *lamenting that no one ever*
> *just "dropped in"*

I was no longer just out of college and looking for a proxy home. I had declared to myself and to the world that my apartment was my base, where I belonged. I at last had something to share with others. Rooms in which they could spread out, a kitchen in which to cook real meals, a dining room table which could stretch large enough so the legs of twelve chairs could fit underneath it and on which my place settings of china (albeit secondhand) could outline the edge of the top of it.

As hard as it was to call one or more homes and arrange an evening, I *made* myself do it at least once every month or six weeks. This was not the five-o'clock, spur-of-the-moment "Why don't you come over to eat?" invitation to one of two or three tried and true single friends. That, although technically "entertaining," was more of an escape from lonely evenings, an impulsive desire to be with someone, than a planned attempt to share my physical surroundings. Such impromptu invitations served their purpose well, enriched many friendships, and saved from oblivion many otherwise forgetable evenings; they did not spur me to clean the bathroom or stack in a corner the shelfless, and in that sense homeless, books (and I sometimes needed this excuse in order to make myself houseclean). They did not give me something to plan for and anticipate, which as the years passed by seemed more and more important—especially on weekends, which could prove long and lonesome.

The rationale for making these formal invitations was more than escape. If I had wanted only escape, I would have been pleased to eat anywhere with anyone; I could have driven five hundred miles to and from my parents' home. The real purpose of these invitations was to fill my hours and my home with purpose and plans, so that escape would eventually seem unnecessary.

The more contented I grew in my own surroundings, the more at ease my parents felt about my leaving them on the Sunday afternoons I did return from their home to mine. I was returning to a place where I and they sensed I belonged. They therefore did not feel responsible for being my home—a situation that, with our growing older, seemed more and more remote and rightfully so.

I was nearly thirty before a test dinner party occurred. Was this home I called mine really mine? For the first time ever I invited my family to my home for a holiday feast. Thanksgiving. Mother, Father, Sister, and Brother-in-law came to celebrate the day. It was not as if the load of the day was entirely on my shoulders. They brought most of the unprepared food—turkey, bread crumbs, potatoes, squash, as well as five different kinds of homemade pie. They were responsible for the basics of the meal.

The food preparation commenced in the morning with the mixing of stuffing—my recipe, not Mother's. I pulled my favorite cookbook from the shelf and proceeded to add its suggested magic combination of spices. Later in the day the same happened with the winter squash and the green beans. Thanksgiving dinner was served according to plan.

But by the second day of the three-day visit, I had tired of being in charge. At mealtimes everyone bowed his or her head and waited—for me. No one prayed until I indicated who should speak to God.

On Friday, when someone eagerly asked, "What's for lunch?" Mother didn't attempt to answer; she expected me to decide which leftovers would be pulled out of the refrigerator.

It seemed to me that mothers, if and when present, should be the managers of such domestic matters. I somehow respected her for not taking over; I probably would have resented it if she had, but her lack of presence depressed me.

I managed quite well in this home of my own when she was out of sight. I had, in the past year, put on several buffets for up to twelve people. It was her voice or the sight of her that sent me back fifteen years to the time when we had been more one female entity than two separate women.

She was no longer allowing me to rest on the comfort of knowing that she would carry responsibility for the holiday traditions, which she or generations before her had made. In my home, whether with my family, my friends, or by myself, I was responsible for establishing my own traditions.

A second answer to the question, "What am I supposed to do with this space now that I've decorated it?" is, "Start establishing traditions."

One should actually start establishing personal traditions and rituals long before the furnishing of a place is near completion.

What is tradition? A "time-honored practice," says *The American Heritage Dictionary.* Traditions are described by sociologist Jay Schvaneveldt as yielding a rightness that comes from repetition.

Traditions and rituals fill ordinary days and weeks with a sense of continuity, but also fill the hours before special days and holidays with anticipation. Although the stereotyped "old maid" may be too rigid in her living habits and rituals, Tevye, in *Fiddler on the Roof,* may have been right in saying, "Without tradition our lives would be as shaky as a fiddler on the roof."

Personal traditions that make a home *yours* may be as

simple as lighting candles at dinnertime, buying yourself flowers once a week, watering the plants in a certain order, baking a pie for every first Sunday of the month, or writing letters one evening a week. Or you may see your traditions as being more holiday-centered—a party on Memorial Day, a cherry cake on Presidents' Day, opening an Advent calendar throughout the Christmas season. Establishing your own traditions for Thanksgiving and Christmas, the traditional "family" holidays, may be a chore that will become an anticipated joy only when circumstances force you to "do it your way"; letting someone else carry the work of making traditions is simply easier than doing it yourself. Being jolted into manufacturing your own less-than-dreamed-of Christmas is difficult, although eventually inevitable.

Every December our family Christmas grew more and more colossal. Mother and Father and children had, over the years, multiplied into thirty people—too many for anyone but one sister to entertain in her larger-than-average house. This particular year two new younger-generation families had been formed: my younger brother and an older sister had each been married. The family was at last paired off—except for me.

Christmas morning I eagerly drove the long trip into the upstate New York countryside. When I arrived, half of the family were there eating the first of the food that would be spread before them continually until bedtime. The flicker of the fireplace and the blinking of the tree lights set the basement family room aglow with the life of Christmas.

I hadn't bought myself a tree. Since my intense Christmas energies were spent here with my family I saved the expense and trauma of setting up a tree by myself. The thought of centering a party around such a detail had never entered my mind.

By one o'clock all thirty people had gathered and Father read the Christmas story. Everyone sat respectfully quiet, but upon the prayer's "Amen" the youngest children yelled "Presents!" as baseball fans yell "Play ball!" on the last note of the pre-game national anthem. Presents. Buffet dinner.

Carol singing around the piano until the children were shuffled off to bed. Games of Scrabble, Uno, and Monopoly until most of the adults had gone to bed and the children had been lifted down to their sleeping bags on the floor. Only three of us were left in the family room, two of my sisters and I. What a good day, I thought. A good old-time Christmas with the addition of cheerful new faces.

And then, the word-bomb was dropped. The bomb that I knew would someday fall and explode my Christmas home, but I wasn't ready for "someday" to come this year.

"You know, the crowd is really getting unwieldly," started one sister. "Entertaining thirty is just more than any of us can handle."

"Well, as the children [my nieces and nephews] get older, we really must all spend our energies on making our own Christmases. Maybe our small family Christmases would be more meaningful if we didn't each have to hurry through them to get here for the second celebration which seems rather superficial anyway. We visit each other during the year, so why is it so important that we all spend Christmas in the same house—or why can't we get together for New Year's?"

Their conversation went on for what seemed like hours. I knew that sooner or later they would notice that I wasn't participating. I kept my eyes steadily on my crocheting, but even so I was making mistakes.

Was I the only one who needed the big celebration, and not on New Year's, on Christmas? How could I be so blind to their exhaustion and they so blind to my desperate need of them, not just of people but of my family on this one day a year?

I felt a version of what Robert Penn Warren called "blood greed":

The child comes home and the parent puts the hooks in him. The old man, or the woman, as the case may be, hasn't got anything to say to the child. All he wants is to have that child sit in a chair for a couple of hours and then go off to bed under the same roof. . . . It is

*just something in the blood. It is a kind of blood greed,
and it is the fate of a man.*

Robert Penn Warren
ALL THE KING'S MEN

One sister finally looked in my direction and, as if I weren't
in the room, said with an embarrassed laugh, "Oh, but what
will Evelyn do?" I did not wish to have them see my pain,
nor did I wish to see their embarrassment. I could not expect
my sisters, who had never lived alone, who had husbands
and children, their own happily nested families, to know
what they were saying or what I was hearing. I let my
crocheting fall to the floor and locked myself behind the
nearest bathroom door.

I sat down on the rug and grieved at the loss of my Christmas dream; I let go of another piece of childhood. I knew
that this would be our last colossal celebration. Some of us
would still gather yearly, but not with such concerted effort.
The words had been spoken—we were adults now. As much
as I wanted to keep things the way they had been, I did not
want Christmas to be an obligation to me.

I was not afraid that I would be left alone; there would
always be a place for me around some or all of my siblings'
trees. But I terribly feared becoming the maiden aunt whom
my nieces and nephews would have to include whether they
wanted to or not. (I had read about such things in novels.)
And I wanted the reverse to be true. I wanted my nieces and
nephews to be flocking to a tree that was mine.

TO MOTHER,
ON THE MAKING OF CHRISTMAS

You silently pass on
to your girl child the magic
mantle of the making.
Are your tears empathy with her
who now must deliver
so heavy a package,
joy that you once again marvel
at the mystery of sugarplums,
or grief that you no longer
bear bows and birds?

Sooner or later, there comes a December when the luxury of being the recipient of an already made Christmas melts and must be molded into the adventure of making one's own gingerbread and scrounging one's own tree decorations— although not necessarily by or for oneself only.

The process may happen gradually, over a period of years. One batch of cookies baked in the communal oven of the YWCA slowly evolved into an apartment decorated with gathered pinecones and a dozen secondhand red ornaments, and later into a festive home fit for hosting a Christmas party.

I tended to think of myself as the only one who found it necessary to keep occupied with work or just plain busyness from December 10 to 25—until the year of my first Christmas party. It was nothing really, a large pot of pasta, a green salad, a chocolate fondue. Entertainment: one guitar-playing friend and seven others who were willing to sing heartily or to laugh at those who were. A smashing success, I was told at the time, and so it seemed, since no one left before 1:00 A.M.

After Christmas, one guest confessed that my party had been her and her husband's real holiday, the one time that year when the warmth of childhood Christmases had returned to their spirits.

I, the maker of someone's Christmas? I laughed at the thought. It was something I hoped to be doing in ten years, but not something I thought I had already done. I had called a party as a selfish diversion; I knew that talking about it, thinking about it, even remembering to thaw the hamburger, would make me less susceptible to December's frostbite.

But a selfish diversion sprouted a tradition, just as my pre-Christmas party had grown into someone's true Christmas.

Although it has not yet happened, there will come a Christmas Day when sickness or snow or poverty will separate me from the company of all my family.

Entertaining myself and friends on the twelve days before Christmas is one thing, but on the day of Christmas it is quite another matter. Some independent women who have tried it swear they will never do it again; others have managed compromises with their expectations.

When it happens to me, I will have to rest in the arms of the friends and on the traditions that I am now building around the day.

The memory of the party I gave two weeks before Christmas, the gingerbread men remaining from the week before, the memory of my childhood Christmases, the assurance of telephone calls, a roast Cornish hen shared with someone as stranded as I, all will fill the hours with contentment.

Filling a house or an apartment with life, your life, will make it home, a place to which you can anticipate going rather than a place you go when there's no other place open.

There will always be days when you want to escape it, just as there were childhood days (probably many) when anywhere looked more exciting than home. Some days the traditions you have built around yourself will seem stifling, and new ones will therefore evolve. The fading curtains and spreads will have to be replaced with livelier-colored fabrics. But when that day comes, when you begin to notice that the colors are not what you once thought they were, you will welcome, not dread, changes that reflect your tastes, interests, and life-style.

EIGHT

A FRIEND OF THE FAMILY?

AWAKENINGS PROMPTED BY TIME

1. Parents
   Upon subtracting and adding,
   my age increases:
   when younger than I
   they conceived me,
   and double my years
   equals more than
   either of theirs.
2. Siblings
   Pink. Rose. Scarlet.
   Tints of one landscape
   as seen through
   six same-colored eyes.

Acceptance of the child my father once was and the man he became comes easier as I get older.
                    Phyllis Naylor, "Strangers"
          THE WASHINGTON POST MAGAZINE
                    January 31, 1982

Nothing is or ever was more wonderful, more dreadful or more inescapable than families, nor are there many more words more perplexing to define. . . . Families breed us, name us, succor us, embarrass us, annoy us, drive us off toward adventures as foreign to them as we can imagine, and then they lure us back.
                    Jane Howard
                    FAMILIES

Father calls me William, sister calls me Will,
Mother calls me Willie, but the fellers call me Bill!
                    Eugene Field
          "Jest 'Fore Christmas"

A home of your own. A few good friends. A sense of security in knowing who you are, what you like and dislike, what you are and are not good at, and an acceptance of God's grace at work in all facets of your personality.

It sounds like the start of a great formula for emotional, if not physical, independence. But what's to be done with the day-to-day or year-to-year working out of the relationships with the family left behind? You may have grown up, made the best of choices as they were laid before you, but your family may or may not have changed at your pace, may or may not have made the discoveries you have.

Must the parent whose spirit you once glimpsed as broken always remain inaccessible to you? Will the parent whom you have forgiven for past mistakes suddenly cease airing opinions that flare up memories you thought were dowsed cold? Must daughters refrain from making decisions of which parents might disapprove? And siblings—what's to be done with long-ago established pecking orders, and more grown-up problems caused by the lack of any common interests? What about the long silences that are kept with the assumption that peace is more to be desired than honesty, or loud fights that occur in the hope that might will make right?

Will we, should we, always be to them what we were as children? The youngest sibling, whom Hilma Wolitzer describes as remaining the "baby" in the eyes of older brothers, sisters, and even of ourselves for the rest of our lives *(Ms.* magazine, January 1982)? The "strong" or "crazy" daughter who went off to the city? The "William," "Will," or "Willie," depending on who is referring to us? Will we always feel, along with the adult daughter, Chelsea, in *On Golden Pond,* that we act grown-up, in control, we even thrive in every environment, every situation—except in the presence of our parents? Should we remain a parent's "little girl," while managing fifteen employees, half of whom are older than ourselves?

"There are few gifts that one person can give to another in this world as rich as understanding," says Rollo May *(The*

Art of Counseling). In that one word, "understanding," and with the tempering imposed on relationships by the passing of time (the new insights and knowledge of each other that come to light) lies the hope of making friends from family.

Their potential for knowing you is greater than that of the best friends made later in life. If each of you can erase the chalk marks of childhood from the others' slates, these people, the ones who actually were with you when your personality was being molded, can be most supportive and helpful in your walk toward a contented, full life.

As much as friends should become as parents and siblings, family should, with time, grow friendlike, family relationships taking on an air of mutuality rather than holding to established roles.

The equality of all is not necessarily the eventual goal of this redefining of relationships; the experience and wisdom of age may always grant the older the prerogative of giving advice to the younger. Or on the other hand the senility of the elderly may call for a child eventually to take over the reins of family responsibility. The ideal goal may be the absence of manipulation—loving, giving, and advising out of concern for one another's well-being, not for the sake of feeding childlike emotional appetites.

Families, although universally praised as the lifeblood of the world, can wreak havoc in the lives of their members. Parents do not let go of their children; children do not let go of their parents; siblings do not let each other outgrow their childhood definitions of each other. Unless specific attempts are made to let go of outdated expectations and to build new relationships on and out of the rubble of the old, a woman's final independence is impossible—the blessed tie that binds may choke.

Only when a woman has truly proven her independence is she able to go back to her family, for a short visit or for a long stay, and remain true to the adult self she has become, true to the home she has emotionally built around herself. She can love them instead of needing them; she can see herself as separate from them, desiring their support, but not being bound to past definitions—to needing their approval, disapproval, or comfort.

My most recent emotional breaking away involved the redefining of an outdated relationship with my younger brother.

With him I "enjoyed" my last child-to-child relationship. As far as I was concerned, he had never grown up; nor had I, when with him. At family gatherings he and I always paired off, often sitting on the sidelines whispering and laughing at our private jokes. We had walked together through fields and woods, talking about dreams of what we someday were going to do and be. Although with Philip I was still a child, it was Philip with whom I had made an old-age pact: If, when retired, either of us had nowhere to go, the other would take in the homeless.

But just prior to his wedding, he started to view himself as a man with responsibilities—as a husband and stepfather-to-be, too responsible for giggling at timeworn silly comments. I strongly suspected that he never noticed that we didn't talk anymore and that he had forgotten our social security agreement. The Philip I had known (and needed) was engulfed in some other, who acted like a stranger.

I would remember his wedding as one remembers a funeral. It was, as far as I could see, my final good-bye to a childhood friend. I sensed that he thought he had outgrown me, that marriage was giving him an insight into life and a responsibility that I in my single state could know nothing about. I defined it as "the arrogance of the married," or conversely, "the patronizing of the single." I was the child he was trying to become older than.

Was the widening rift completely his fault? No. I was guilty of wanting to hold on to a relationship that constricted us to the past; I wanted to keep him in a pigeonhole that he had outgrown. Time would have to redefine our positions and allow them to settle on a different plane—where we both understood each other in the present, but in the light of the past.

Life marches by, Chelsea, I suggest you get on with it.
Ethel Thayer to her
daughter, Chelsea
ON GOLDEN POND

Carol counted as valuable the encounters—whether good or bad—she had with her only brother. He could and did confront her, without her feeling threatened. She did not see him as making stabs at her past; since they had grown from the same root, been nurtured from the same soil, he could not mock or challenge her base without ridiculing his own. They had lived through the wonderful but horrible years of childhood in the same house and thus shared a basic understanding of each other's scars and outlook on life.

She saw his occasional "What are you doing with your life?" questions as "tough medicine," but necessary to her sorting out her own priorities. When they talked about their separate perceptions of their mutual past, she usually saw the memories, or the people who moved in and out of the memories, in a brighter light. She saw the situation more through the eyes of the adult she had become than through the eyes of the child who had experienced it.

Carol did not see her brother as influencing her in a way that involved power—he challenged her, he did not load her with false guilt and unwarranted fears.

Families have no more power than their members allow them. They can make us loathe both the parts of ourselves that have been or are replicas of their flaws, and the faults they viewed as foreign to themselves and thus intolerable. But it is up to us to break or not to break any constricting chains that make us feel guilty, less than worthy, or overly dependent on their presence, approval, or disapproval. Divesting them of their power involves more than forgiveness, it means seeing them as no more powerful or weak than ourselves, as no more mortal or immortal than ourselves, as speakers of words that are no more devastating, consoling, angering, or exhilarating than the words we speak to them or to others.

My problem was not my mother. My problem was myself. When I stopped giving her the power to make me unhappy or angry, she could no longer hurt me and I could love her and accept the kind of love she was able to give me.
Bruce Larson
THERE'S A LOT MORE TO HEALTH THAN NOT BEING SICK

A family's basic temperament may never mellow, but because our inner attitudes change, we may be able to grow away from them—become independent of them—and *then* return, to love them.

Mothers, especially, may be threatened by their daughters finally "growing up" and no longer needing them as their little girls once did. The old role of comfort-giver or guilt-layer or fear-sharer may fill the mothers' need to be needed. Their empty birdhouse may be a black home darker than they care to walk into. They may somehow rationalize that if they can still mother their single daughters, they have a niche of their own.

Maybe they can or should "mother" their now adult daughters, but whether or not they do need not and should not be of life-or-death consequence to their independent daughters.

The question took me by surprise: If I knew that my parents would only live one more year, would I move back home or close enough to them that I could visit them daily or weekly?

I answered "No," and quickly qualified it with, "Not for my own benefit, but I would go if I knew they needed me."

I could hardly believe that answer had come from my throat. I felt guilty. I should, I thought, want to rush to their sides and soak in every available minute of their presence. Then I would have one more year of memories, advice, counsel, and love to lean back on when time stole them from the other end of the phone line.

The thirty-one-year-old woman who asked me the question lived five hundred miles from her parents' home. She thought she would go to them if she knew for sure that one or the other would be gone by her thirty-second birthday. "The thought that I would go on living after they were dead just makes me sick. All those years of missing them would be ahead of me, and I would have passed by a chance to have a year of good times with them."

For me, I would miss them—to what extent I will not know until the day or days are thrust upon me. The moment of our good-byes will not be as black as I had once imagined. It will not be as wrenching as the farewell my thirteen-year-old niece had envisioned for herself on Ellis Island. I will not feel as utterly alone and therefore as hysterical as I was when I first saw *Fiddler on the Roof*, identifying myself with Tevye's daughter Hodel when she was leaving her family, going to Siberia to make a home of her own. Her good-byes to her father, at a blustery, barren train stop, were as final as death. Hodel was crossing the bar into another world. It was clear she would never again see her family.

Then, at age eighteen, I viewed myself as my parents' daughter but saw into the future far enough to know that it would not always be so. If I were the daughter of someone who no longer lived and breathed, would my breath be stolen from me?

> *The great theme is not Romeo and Juliet. . . . The great theme we all share is that of becoming ourselves, of overcoming our father and mother, of assuming our identities somehow.*
>
> Anne Sexton
> *ANNE SEXTON: A SELF-PORTRAIT IN LETTERS*

My questions, in ten years, have changed. In my conscious and subconscious mind I carry with me the accumulated years of my parents' teaching, their example, their concern, their priorities, their tastes, their idiosyncracies—whether good or bad.

These parts of them that have become parts of me are no longer necessarily connected to their physical beings. Time has been the great sorter-outer. Which parts of them *should* be significant parts of me?

When I first left them every step was an experiment in keeping my balance. In this situation, would the I who was separate from them naturally react as they had reacted, or would I find purpose, delight, and fulfillment in some circles, some mode of service, some environment, or mind-set different from theirs yet always influenced by them?

Many parents, blind to the separateness of their children, see that three must forever remain as one. Fathers are convinced that they are cutting a trail for their children to follow. Parents insist that children will finish all of college, whether they want to or not. Parents are deeply hurt when their children join a denomination different from theirs, molding the future into some shape other than what they had envisioned. They had seen their children as adults who would, who must, physically and emotionally rally around them, the aged parents.

But I look at the Bible story of Joseph, son of Jacob. In a land and with a life-style hardly imaginable to his father, Joseph carried out God's word to him, which ultimately brought about God's purposes for his people. It was not the plan Jacob would have seen as obvious, nor was it the plan that allowed Jacob the pleasure or pride of shepherding, leading, and protecting Joseph through hard times. Until he was a very old man, Jacob could not brag about his successful son, nor relive the dreams of his own youth through the life of this, his favorite child; Jacob thought Joseph was dead.

And Joseph, apart from and without his family's reminders of expectations, did not forget what he had learned as a child.

The parts of himself that Jacob would have been most proud of lived on in Egypt, in the child who was separated from him, more than in many of the children who spent their whole lives near his tent.

In the long run, leaving home might have made growing up easier for Joseph than for his siblings. From long distance he nurtured the part of Jacob that really was a part of or compatible with his own nature.

Although Joseph was obviously overjoyed and moved when he was reunited with his brothers and then his father, he did not rush to spend every waking hour with elderly Jacob so that he could glean more truths and insights from the wisdom of age. He generously provided for his father's care; he traveled to Jacob's deathbed and it seems his concern was Jacob-centered rather than self-centered. He gave his family more than they gave him.

"But I can't," you might say. "I can't handle a life where I am not, in some fashion, dependent on people I am certain are stronger than I."

I held out on one issue—I could not buy a car for myself. Although I have always paid the invoice, Father has negotiated each deal and the details of registration. He has told me where to pick up the car and where to sign my name on the papers. Walking into a showroom (where I am assumed ignorant, whether I am or not) and then allowing my ignorance to slip through my nervous facade so that the salesman smirks at discovering that he was right all along, is more humiliation than I care to confront.

I childishly and unashamedly asked Dad to take this responsibility off my hands. "Father, I can't," I said.

But upon more careful inspection, "I can't" seemed an obvious and easy excuse and misuse of words. Nothing physically stopped me from shopping and buying for myself. I simply didn't want to battle one more monster that looked larger than I. "Father, I don't want to" was a more correct complaint.

In similar fashion, the "I can't" of viewing a family through adult eyes may more accurately be defined as "I don't care to go through the painful process of letting go."

The time will never come when parents are not missed. When a young teen, I remember overhearing a fifty-year-old grandmother tell my mother how depressed she grew at times because she missed her mother, who had died. About that same time I puzzled at seeing my father, whom I viewed as wholly self-sufficient and separate from his parents, sobbing at his mother's casket. I recently read a magazine article describing a scene in which a young girl walked in on her middle-aged mother who was silently staring out of the window, crying. The woman explained to her daughter that she was lonely for her own mother, who had died long before the child had been born. The girl, identifying herself as the motherless daughter, started crying empathetically. One will always grieve and feel alone at the thought of being a motherless or fatherless child. But the parent we have cultivated within ourselves will stay with us and comfort us through our own old age.

How then should we act toward parents and siblings who are more friends than authority?

Lois, age thirty-two, lived thirty miles from her parents' home. The stormy years were past. She felt assured of who she was. Yet her father, like a watchdog, hovered over the engine of her car. She couldn't possibly take care of it herself, he thought. Mechanics would take advantage of her; they would destroy what he and his serviceman had maintained.

She had grown tired of his distrust, resenting his "fathering." Of course she could take her car to the local station and have the necessary work done. It would take her less time; money wasn't a problem and besides, he would be free of the responsibility. Until—she stepped back from the situation enough to see the pleasure he received from giving to her, from taking a responsibility off her shoulders and on to his. It was the only area of her life he interfered with. Why should she resent his offer when he actually was trying to help her? Was independence for the sake of independence her goal?

She had established her separateness, her ability to survive. She was director of personnel for a small corporation. She owned her own condominium. She sat on many church decision-making committees.

She sensed her own pleasure in giving her father and mother gifts of herself—conversation, assurances that they were not alone. She foresaw when they might need more of her than they currently did. The tables would eventually turn. Someday their age might make them dependent on her resources. They knew that as well as she did.

So now, when they were all able-bodied, able-minded adults, why should they not "freely give" to each other the gifts they had separately cultivated? Why shouldn't she be grateful that the car was all her father meddled with, and accept his concern with thanks?

My parents generously supply me with the bounty of their garden, their cupboards, their years of collecting and crafting household items. If I accept their gifts, am I resorting to an unhealthy, childlike dependence? Not if it is given as a gift of love with no strings attached, and if I stay aware of the fact that I must not ask for or expect their contributions.

If the gifts were not given on a continuous basis, could I take care of those needs myself? If so, I should receive gladly, give openheartedly in return, and enjoy our years of mutuality.

Gift giving *and* receiving can go awry with selfish motives. Some independent women are moving back home, blaming the economy for the unpaid utility bills, all the while spending $40 a week on restaurant lunches. On the other hand, some parents are selfish in their giving.

One can dominate others through gifts.

Paul Tournier
THE MEANING OF GIFTS

Carol Anne struggled through a difficult phone conversation. No. She had no intention of going to her parents' for Christmas. Her childhood memories of the day haunted her. She did not want to be forced into another ugly holiday. She wanted to spend this day with friends. Her parents were informing her that they had already made and paid for her cross-country plane reservations. "We've taken care of everything," they assured her.

This was no gift of garden vegetables. Their gift had long ropes attached. The reservations had been made before Carol Anne had been asked if she would like to come home. In return for their gift of so many dollars of air fare, they were asking for so many hours of holiday time. It was not as if they would otherwise be spending Christmas alone; the other children were coming home. Her parents wanted Carol Anne to join them; they were forcing her to join them.

Carol Anne said she would love to take up their offer if it were transferred to the Thanksgiving holiday, which was not, in her mind, crowded with ghosts. They thought Carol Anne was being unreasonable and ungrateful. Carol Anne thought they were being manipulative . . . and so the tearful conversation continued. She held out, saying she would not come on their conditions.

Gifts: Given out of love? Given out of need? Received out of love? Received out of need?

The combinations made by connecting these four phrases can prove deadly or healthy, damning or freeing, draining or full of life.

> *We must love them both, those whose opinions we share and those whose opinions we reject. For both have labored in the search for truth and both have helped us in the finding of it.*
>
> Thomas Aquinas

> *To resent them was to resent my own choice to be different from them, a choice that I was happy with.*
>
> M. Scott Peck
> *THE ROAD LESS TRAVELED*

They grow older, and maybe wiser. Parents who once confidently directed their children's lives, parents who once firmly voiced disapproval of their children's style of living, often come to a point where love and appreciation for respect and kindnesses win out over attitudes of judgment. I asked one friend about her parents' attitude toward her disregard for the church, which had been her parents' life and vocation.

"They're glad I'm alive and healthy," she answered.

Of course they pray earnestly that their child will someday find an assurance of salvation akin to their own. But neither party spoils the memory of infrequent visits with arguments that no one ever wins.

For Monica, the thoughts of caring for her parents when they were old were so confining that she could never conjure up the scene in her mind. Like bats, the thoughts occasionally darted through her consciousness but they never, never stopped and rested. Although she did not have a large house, as did her siblings, she was the only one who was single and in that sense free of entangling responsibilities. Her freedom might make it easier for her to "give up" her life for them than for her sisters to give up theirs.

If a family meeting were ever called to decide on such

matters, she didn't know what she would do. No matter what might transpire, she felt she would walk away feeling badly. If she didn't volunteer, she would be overcome with guilt; if she did volunteer, she would make the offer in martyrdom, not out of genuine love or desire to be a servant.

A dramatic change of heart came as part of her spiritual journey—one of those changes which seems a natural next step. She was at an otherwise forgettable church service, but the Word's voice to her personally spoke loud and clear, and it came in the form of a reassurance. Yes, she might very well be asked to take on the responsibility she most hated thinking about, but if and when that day came she would be ready; the grace of God would accompany the task. Grace would abound, but only when she needed it. Then it would replace the dread—the confines that even now constricted her spirit.

What gift can we give both our families and ourselves that will relieve all of us of unhealthy lifelong ties?

Might the secret lie in the suspension of judgments? In not judging so that we will not be judged? In letting our families see the strong and the frail sides of our personalities? Over the years Ruth phoned home not only to relieve her frustrations and release her emotions—to ask for more parenting—but also to reach out in love to those who had given her years of care. She helped them in ways she never before thought appropriate for daughter/mother or daughter/father relationships. She foresaw the day when she might feel she should hold her crying mother or advise her parents or older siblings who had always given her advice.

It was Bruce Larson's grown children who suggested it was time he quit playing his life to his mother *(There's a Lot More to Health Than Not Being Sick)*. And so might we all be called to return to our families as whole people, known to them for our love.

At least we were given the opportunity to grow up.
An independent woman

When I was a child, my speech, my outlook, and my thoughts were all childish. When I grew up, I had finished with childish things. Now we see only puzzling reflections in a mirror, but then we shall see face to face. My knowledge now is partial; then it will be whole, like God's knowledge of me. In a word, there are three things that last for ever: faith, hope, and love; but the greatest of them all is love.

1 CORINTHIANS 13:11-13, NEB

NINE

▭

NEVER QUITE THERE?

GOING HOME:
A DREAM'S UNANSWERED QUESTIONS

I travel by square oak breadboard
bolted to piano wheels,
powered by my heels
when I sit on it,
hands and toes
when I lie with it pressed
against my lower ribs.
The ground gained
passes under me, but hardly
in proportion to the energy I expend—
(stones rooting in the road,
often uphill, and the miles
numbering in three digits).
Haven't I already journeyed
this one-way route
and long ago reached
my destination: haven.
So why does this sleep's struggle
deny my arrival?

When I was nearly finished with this book, a deep depression settled over me. I had just told the world that I have at my disposal all the ingredients necessary for a contented life, yet I felt, for that week anyway, anything but satisfied.

I was confronted with close friends leaving town, the landlady putting my apartment up for sale, my employment uncertain as the writing of the book had occupied most of my days for nearly six months, a birthday (which I had tried to ignore) making its presence unmistakably known.

I felt uprooted and at a loss to know what could or should be next. The comfortable home I thought I had built around me was oh, so necessary, but physically shakier than I had imagined. Was this tangible home that gave my life structure and rest an inadequate pill that dissolved pain but cured no disease? Would the desire for permanence and the security of long-term commitments to people and to places occasionally, forever, beckon? Would there always be days when I would feel, along with Patricia Houck Sprinkle, "homesick for all the homes I have ever known" *(Daily Guideposts, 1981)?*

If friends vanished from sight, if I moved my possessions into rooms that didn't suit me as much as these, if I did not continue in employment that was challenging, if birthdays started arriving more than once a year, would I find myself as insecure and as uncertain of my capabilities, my likes and dislikes, my identity as I was on my college graduation day? Would I feel as homeless as I then did?

As much as I can never go back to the naive all-consuming physical and emotional security of childhood, I can never go back to the days when confidence and self-knowledge were foreign-vocabulary words. Today is built on the understanding and wisdom gained by having walked through yesterday. I can face today's obstacles knowing that yesterday's looked as large or larger than these; if they proved surmountable, will not today's also be?

What has time given to me? What does time give to any independent woman?

A perspective that enlightens. A memory that strengthens.

I remember the first time I drove alone on an expressway. That sleepy Sunday morning's traffic would not now threaten my sense of safety or tax my judgment, but then it seemed as hazardous and risky as taking the reins of an unbroken horse.

I remember my brother's first-grade daughter staring at me, aghast, when I once told her that I lived alone. Her eyes revealed horror at the thought of empty rooms, which her mind translated into empty hours. But possessing the only keys to an apartment has not proven a weight heavier than I can bear. Having once lived alone and survived forever takes the fear out of again walking through that door.

Having learned to conquer new skills and working relationships makes the next challenges maybe no less awesome, but manageable, or, if not manageable, it makes the alternatives seem not so dreadful or final.

I've gained the knowledge that sometimes self-respect comes only by gambling—by setting your eyes on what you want and then reaching for it. Tennyson's view of love:

> 'Tis better to have loved and lost
> Than never to have loved at all.

might well be transferred to life in general:

> Better to have tried and failed
> Than never to have tried.

Employment opportunities, prospective loves, possible avenues of service—all have provided situations where women have said, "I would have hated myself if I hadn't tried. I would have been haunted, always wondering what might have been."

Age gives and time or circumstance cannot steal the courage and faith of knowing that if something looks as if it is what and where your spirit truly wants to be, if it is in keeping with God's guidelines, then you should, you must, open every possible door and begin to walk toward that goal.

Time gives a knowledge of what one is willing to work for or endure. Age, the immediate result of the passing of time, gives an acquaintance of mine who is in her mid-thirties the right to hint to her mid-twenties roommate (who has her life "together" and her career path mapped out as neatly as a Triptik) that time is an unseen and unpredictable force that may change the desirability or possibility of one's best-laid intentions. It also gives people who are thirty years older than I the right to suggest that I still have much to discover about finding a home that is indestructible.

Life grows easier, yet never easy. When I stop and look at the long-term growth, I know that one is foolish to consider the ups and downs of individual days. One should look at the healing and wholeness that spread wider and longer over the span of years.

The home I carry with me continues to struggle with the parts of itself, the rooms, that it feels are decorated in some fashion that is less than suited to my tastes. Yes, in my dreams I still struggle to get somewhere beyond where I am—to get closer and closer to home.

But we are asked to walk in the light we have been given. I cannot physically cover my walls with prints I have not yet discovered or with remembrances of memories I have not yet made; I cannot force emotional or spiritual wisdom to ripen when it is still a new, small bud.

Home—the place where I am comfortable—grows larger with time, with strength, with the assurance of God's defining love. The kingdom of God grows larger inside me, and the Lord becomes my dwelling place (Ps. 90:1).

I recently pulled out from a desk drawer an essay I wrote several years ago. The intensity of those feelings is behind me, but the ultimate answer to my restlessness remains unchanged. A heavenly Father will live in me, and from him there need be no breaking away, no redefining of relationship, no change that comes with time.

"Eating?"

"No. We just finished," he said. "What's up?"

My telltale silence told him nothing was up; everything was up. After ten seconds that seemed like five minutes I managed a short, "Just felt like calling you." After another, shorter silence I said, "How's everybody there?"

"Carol's working tonight. She and the girls are fine," my brother said. "I have a cold but I'm still teaching. Oh, you should have been here last night. The hot-water heater sprang a leak. We didn't notice it until water was halfway across the family room floor. We've been drying out all day. What about you? Still hanging in there?"

I tapped my right clinched fist against the arm of the rocker, trying to think of what to say and how. "I just can't stand this," I blurted. "If I have to come home to this empty apartment one more night, I'm going to go crazy." There, I had said it. But . . . "Well, it's not just that. It's that this friend of mine, Amy, needs help tonight and wants me to fold and collate some monthly newsletters for the singles group at her church. You know, I can't think of anything I'd hate more than folding newsletters this evening—except maybe staying home in this attic alone. Those are my two options for tonight. Some choice!"

This time the silence was on his end. Then he started, "You know I would come over if I could. Maybe long distance is the next best thing to being there, but sometimes I know it's not good enough. And the distance is too long. I remember—I really do—some of those winter nights when I was in Kentucky and Carol and the whole family were in New York. Phone calls weren't good enough. Keeping myself occupied didn't work. I walked the block again and again, kicking the stones on the street saying, 'God, it's so lonely.'

"I'm with you, Sis. That probably doesn't sound like much when you're still sitting there alone. And I'm not sure I'd be excited about folding newsletters either. Work doesn't always fill the gap."

By this time I was a mess. My whole face was red and wet, and I was shaking and rocking back and forth. There was nothing more I could say. I only managed, "Look. I think I'd better go while I can still say good-bye . . . and thanks."

"Wait a minute," he said. "I want you to know that I'm thinking about you all evening. Not worrying about you, just thinking of you and feeling sad with you."

I hung up the phone, put my feet up on the edge of the chair seat, and sobbed for twenty minutes, sobbed with the assurance that someone was holding me even though he wasn't in the same room. He hadn't told me "Buck up," hadn't told me things would get better when he had no way of knowing they would, hadn't become fretful and worried about my spiritual and emotional stability—he had just said, "I'm with you."

Half an hour after dialing the phone I went into the kitchen and cooked the first good meal I'd had in a week:

baked chicken with rice and peas. Later I drove to the church and spent an hour licking stamps and putting them on folded newsletters.

I came home early, tired and ready for bed. As I was flipping off the bedside lamp, parts of two Bible verses slid into my mind:

"There is a friend who sticks closer than a brother"
(PROVERBS 18:24).

"Surely he has . . . carried our sorrows"
(ISAIAH 53:4).

We grow up. We grow away; we grow less dependent on our families and more dependent on the God who never changes, who asks that we always remain as children in our approach to him. He asks that we be secure in the promise that we are in the process of being molded into the likeness of his Son— in the process of finding our spiritual home.

Our Father, even as we speak the word "Father" we acknowledge your claims upon us and our dependence upon you. We do not like to think of ourselves as children, but as men and women who are on top of things, acting rather than reacting, speaking rather than listening, teaching rather than learning. And yet you have said, "Except you become as little children, you shall not enter into the kingdom."

Keep, somehow, the child in each of us alive, wonderfilled, responsive to all about us, quick to laugh when there is reason to laugh, able to weep when we need to weep, confident of a father's unquestioned ability to make it all come out right.

But there is more to life—and faith—than childhood. Be now to [us] wisdom and strength, energy and patience, vision and faithfulness.

. . . We thank you for all who have gone before, and trust you for all who shall come after. Amen.

Kenneth L. Wilson